H. M. Koutoukas
1937–2010

Remembered by His Friends

Edited by Magie Dominic & Michael Smith

The cover image is the set design by Donald L. Brooks for *Christopher at Sheridan Squared*.

The photograph on the title page is by Lisa Jane Persky.

The photographs by Peter Hujar on pages 59 and 68 and the back cover are copyright © 1987 by The Peter Hujar Archive LLC. Courtesy of Matthew Marks Gallery, New York.

The photographs by James D. Gossage opposite page 1 and on pages 4, 13, 15, 19, 52, and 63 are the property of the photographer.

ISBN 978-0-9794736-6-1

Copyright © 2010 by Magie Dominic & Michael Smith

Fast Books, P. O. Box 1268, Silverton, OR 97381

Contents

Magie Dominic eulogy	1
Michael Ellick sermon	6
Robert Heide interview	10
Donald Brooks remembrance	28
We Were So Young Once (poem)	37
Penny Arcade remembrance	38
Lisa Jane Persky remembrance	40
Koutoukas Plays Binghamton	47
Binghamton Press obituary	49
Cookie Mueller interview	50
Brief comments	58
Yoko Ono	
James Rado	
Jean-Claude van Itallie	
Jim Gossage	
Ann Harris	
Walter Harris	
Marjorie Lipari	
Mel England	
Maggie Low	
Stephen Koch	
Heather Rose Dominic	
Robert Patrick	
Bob Shields	
Michael Smith poem	67
Documentation	69

Photo by James D. Gossage

H. M. Koutoukas and Magie Dominic at the opening of the Caffè Cino exhibition at the Library of the Performing Arts at Lincoln Center, March 5, 1985.

Eulogy to H. M. Koutoukas
by Magie Dominic

Delivered at H.M.Koutoukas Memorial Mass on March 28, 2010, at Judson Memorial Church in New York City.

My friendship with Harry Koutoukas began almost half a century ago—at the Caffè Cino. I don't believe the Harry we knew and loved would ever have existed without the artistic freedom of the Caffè Cino. I would never have existed. We were safe there. The Cino existed for a ten-year window of time—1958-1968—and what transpired there changed the face of world theatre.

For Harry, the years 1964-1967 were pivotal. In little more than three years he wrote and produced the following plays:

—In 1964, *Only a Countess May Dance When She's Crazy* and *Turtles Don't Dream*.

—In 1965, *All Day for a Dollar, or Crumpled Christmas; Medea, or Maybe the Stars May Understand; A Letter from Colette, or Dreams Don't Send Valentines; Tidy Passions, or Kill, Kaleidoscope, Kill; Michael Touched Me; Two Camps by Koutoukas* (*The Last Triangle, an Embroidered Camp*, and a revival of *Only a Countess May Dance When She's Crazy*), off-Broadway at the Actors Playhouse; *With Creatures Make My Way*; and the opera *Pomegranada*, with music by Al Carmines, at Judson Poets Theatre. Almost inconceivable. That same year he received the National Arts Club Award for Experimental Playwriting; and *Turtles Don't Dream* was produced at Carnegie Hall.

—In 1966, *Cause Célèbre* and *Cobra Invocations*. That year he received an Obie Award for both playwriting and production.

—In 1967, *When Clowns Play Hamlet*. Harry directed most of his own plays.

Whenever a show canceled at the Caffè Cino, something had to be improvised on short notice. Several memorable shows were done with comic books as the script. If you put Marcel Marceau, Mozart, Charlie Chaplin, and Kate Smith all in a bottle and shake it, the genie that comes out will be comic book drama. The very first comic book production was *Wonder Woman*, in 1966, with Harry in the title role.

In August 1967, we did *Snow White*, and I was Snow White. It was like playing tag. You're "it." And the race is on. The room was packed. The audience had already arrived for the nine o'clock show. In the dressing room Harry was in flowing robes, with scarves and jewels and full make-up as the evil queen. I was wearing whatever I'd been wearing as I walked down the street that night, but a wedding gown had been assembled in a matter of minutes by someone and was ready for that happy ending.

The artist Kenny Burgess was draped in fur and feathers as all the forest animals. Playwrights and strangers were dwarfs. The prince was handsome. Charles Stanley was the magic mirror and did lights and sound. The Royal Huntsman had just arrived from Fire Island. Everything had been arranged in a matter of minutes. In the fleeing-through-the-forest scene Bob Patrick waved gigantic ferns as if he were being chased by demons. Charles created a lightning storm with a blaring aria. I raced across the stage, back and forth, until I collapsed, fourteen times a week, for two weeks. More than two hundred people were dwarfs; every performance they were different and the number was always changing. In the death-to-the-evil-queen scene, the dwarfs grabbed pastries from a tray in the kitchen and fired cannolis, éclairs, and napoleons as if they were hand grenades, and His Majesty Harry Koutoukas, the evil queen, swooned under a mountain of whipped cream and pastry. That was comic book drama.

For the next thirty years Harry continued to write and produce work in virtually every Off-Off-Broadway venue. His writing style is featured in countless books and reviews. His

Photo courtesy of Donald L. Brooks

H. M. Koutoukas in the title role of "Wonder Woman" at the Caffè Cino, with Deborah Lee, 1966.

work is extravagant, imaginative, and tender.

In 2003 he received the Chesley Playwriting Award from The Publishing Triangle in New York. My book was nominated for an award that same night but it didn't win; Harry told me they would call in the morning and tell me they'd made a mistake!

In the past decade, books about the Caffè Cino have started to appear, some of them accurate, some of them hopelessly wrong. I complained to Harry one day that people were getting the story wrong, dates were wrong, conversations were inaccurate. Harry told me not to worry; he said I'd always have a job, getting it right.

Photo by James D. Gossage

Mary Boylan, Robert Dahdah, and H. M. Koutoukas with his famous parrot at the performance of "Tender Tales," Coda Gallery, 1965.

Harry adored tradition and ritual. He loved Christmas and Valentine's and birthdays. One year, in the mid-sixties, I made a small cardboard sign with red glitter and the words *Harry's birthday is June 4th!* It hung on the Cino wall for two years. When the café closed in 1968, boxes of posters and photos were taken to Lincoln Center by Michael Smith. Jim Gossage gave an entire archive of photographs. In 1985 I co-curated an exhibition at Lincoln Center and researched hundreds of dates, names, and productions. In one of the boxes was a fragile cardboard sign, with tarnished red glitter, announcing the birthday of Harry Koutoukas.

This week (May 2010) I visited Lincoln Center Research Library. The Caffè Cino poster from the 1985 exhibit happened to be on display on the main floor as part of an amazing poster display of Lincoln Center exhibitions. I went upstairs to check the card catalogue for Harry documentation. There were only a few entries so far. One of the three cards under his name reads the following: *H. M. Koutoukas birthday card made by Magie Dominic.* That little piece of the Cino wall, Harry's home, still exists and has its own catalogue number within the archives of Off-Off-Broadway at Lincoln Center.

Harry and I didn't spend a lot of time on the telephone. We wrote letters to each other, and postcards. At holidays and birthdays and Christmas and for no special occasion at all. I wrote long letters with glitter and photos and stars enclosed. Harry would send a postcard with a line or two of poetry or something about what was going on in his life. On one of his postcards he wrote:

The sun came out as I took your card out of the mailbox.
Hope summer is treating you well.
All for art, Koutoukas

Harry was a flamboyant, awe-inspiring giant of a genius, but there was also another Harry. A fragile spirit, a lover of butterflies and the delicate creatures of nature. A complicated monarch-butterfly type of person. Keep that image of Harry safe. Alongside the showy, cape-wearing, rhinestone-wearing, fast-talking genius playwright, there also existed a brilliant fragile butterfly who received his intricate wings at a tiny storefront theatre nearly a half century ago. Harry was a cheerleader for the rest of the world—which is probably why so many people have so many memories of his compassion, his kindness, his genuine interest in your life.

Harry really did mean it when he said you were special. Because you were, and you are, and he knew that.

Michael Ellick Sermon
at Judson Memorial Church
March 7, 2010

I wanted to talk a little bit more about Harry and what happened last night, not only because I know so many of you want to know everything that I know, but because religiously I believe this is far more spiritually instructive than anything I could think out and then say. First I want to give a little background about Harry Koutoukas, for those of you who don't know. Harry M. Koutoukas was a playwright and he was a great mind. An example is, Harry founded the School of Gargoyles. It's not a traditional school, it's a school of thought. Because Harry said that gargoyles had the ability to see the world and use language in a new way. He was one of the leaders of the original Off-Off-Broadway movement in the sixties, and his work always spoke to the gritty truth or hyper-irony of Harry's point of view, which was always delivered on his own terms. Likewise, Harry seemed to know everybody. He was like next door neighbors and best friends with Yoko since she moved to the city, and Harvey Fierstein used to pay him all this money to teach him how to write plays. Everyone has a lot of stories and there is going to be a lot of chance to share them. Harry was also, I might add, my friend, and he was a scoundrel.

Well, yesterday, Harry died. Harry died in the early hours of Saturday morning. We don't think it was suicide, basically certain. We don't know exactly how he died. Most likely there was some kind of a complication with his medication, we don't know for sure, but yesterday at five o'clock his friend Jana found him, at his apartment, and she called the EMTs, and they came, and immediately they pronounced him dead. And she waited there with some other friends who showed up, and eventually she got Donna's number, and Diana called me, and Diana called Hastings in the back. So I went over, and I had an

Photo by Heather Rose Dominic

opportunity to be with Harry, on the floor of his bedroom, and I gave him last rites. And I sat there with his friends, and we laid hands on him, and we prayed, and we cried and we told stories, and then Hastings showed up, and we told more stories, and we cried and we laughed and we prayed some more. Do you want to share anything about last night? *[Voice: Only that it was sacred, funny, laughing, crying, just what you're saying, and he would have been proud of the send-off. It was very theatrical.]* I actually want to illustrate how theatrical it was. We were there for hours. And when the people finally came to take his body out, we had one last minute to pray and say goodbye, and so we all did the thing where we held hands and had our hands on him, and we said something, goodbye, and it was touching and moving, and then at some point, I can't remember the guy's name, he had this clarity about him, right there in this intimate moment, over Harry's body, to start *[claps his hands]*, so we all started doing it, we started clapping *[claps]*, and we cried "Bravo!" as they carried his body out. And then we were downstairs, and they had all these live flowers from his table, that he'd had out, and we threw flowers at this poor man, and we were on Christopher

Street, "Bravo!" *[claps]*, and we're throwing, strewing flowers about, and I thought, boy, if you've got to go, this is how you do it. *[Voice: Say about the policeman.]* And there was this policeman who had to sit there and wait, you know, from when the EMTs come to when the morgue comes, and I guess he's a pretty cute guy *[Voice: Very cute guy]*, very cute guy, and the entire time we're doing all this he's there, he does this all the time, and we're kind of getting off on, here this guy is sitting on Harry's bed, and how perfect, what a short little play this is, that Harry could not have constructed better himself. There was the air of synchronicity and magic about everything that happened last night. So I wanted to share that with you. We're going to have a lot of time to talk about Harry and reflect on his life, and of course we're going to do it in campy over-the-top style, and you just wait and see it.

Because of circumstances and time, I'm not going to give the sermon I had planned, but I am going to paraphrase a little bit of the very last page of it, because it is so very poignant and maybe perfect. I find it very odd that I was going to preach on finding the sacred in the profane, because of course, that was Harry. The nine different bulletin covers you find around here was not just a campy, sneaky tactic to get you sharing them all with each other and talking with each other, it was also a kind of a silly way to remind us of something very simple—that most of us do not experience spirituality through religion anymore. Rather, we experience spirituality, if any, through a referential hall of arts and media that our society has become, and that's very Harry too. And I was going to talk about how, theologically and socially, this might be a good thing, and about what happened at churches, like this one, in the 1960s, when they started looking for the divine outside of the constructs of their traditions and their church walls, and not only how they looked at first to artists and playwrights and painters and singers to show them where the spirit moved, but what they learned about overthrowing the political and religious establishment through a spectacle of pop culture. That's what my sermon was going to be about. And if you know Harry, I was going to talk about how amazing it is that we get to have a drag queen named Ruby Rims do our children's blessing and lead us in worship. And why our special music today, after the sermon, is going to be led by a musical theatre post-punk band named the Gay Agenda doing a mash-up of Mama Cass, Jay Z, Britney Spears, Miley Cyrus, and Lady Gaga, and how awesome that is, and how sacred that is, and how important it is for churches like Judson to continue to challenge themselves as the research and development laboratory of American Christianity. I was even going to announce—I guess I'm still going to do it—the formation of a laboratory for theological spectacle here at Judson. This is something Mike and I have been talking about for a while to Donna—the formation of an artistic think tank, a pop lab that reacts to the big questions of religion and politics in a new context. The point is that the service that Mike and I spent a lot of time thinking about and scratching our heads about, strangely, is also an entirely appropriate reflection on and lesson from our friend Harry Koutoukas. Because as I knew him, at his core was the hope that each of us could be free from the authorities that inhibit us, whether they be religious authorities, who tell us what you're supposed to believe, or whether they be pop culture authorities, who tell you how you're supposed to look, what you're supposed to wear, what you're supposed to buy, and what your play is supposed to be about. Well, as Harry might say, screw that, darlings. Inside each of us, underneath all the acts and the pretense and the trying to fit in. there is something beautiful, something holy and sacred in the gritty, unedited truth of each person, something divine in the silliness and the camp of it, something sacred in the horror and the humor of all the in-between moments of our lives, and it's not enough to just hum that tune inside your head, you've actually got to work to make your own kind of music, and you've got to own it and celebrate it and work it and above all you've got to love it.

So that, my darlings, is my prayer for you today.
Amen.

All About Harry

an interview with H. M. Koutoukas
by Robert Heide

(from the New York Native, October 29, 1990)

Before Bette Midler called herself "The Divine Miss M," and before there was the great late Divine of *Pink Flamingos* fame, there was "The Divine H. M.," sometimes known to friends and theatrical cohorts as Harry H. M. Koutoukas (the initials are meant to stand for His Majesty) who came to Greenwich Village where he has lived for over thirty years. I first met him at the Rienzi coffee shop on MacDougal Street in the early 1960s, then again later at the Caffè Cino, the first little theatre to describe itself as "Off-Off-Broadway," where we were both writing and producing our plays under the aegis of Joe Cino.

On Sheridan Square and on Christopher Street in those days, Harry could often be seen elaborately garbed and searching for the legendary lost Cobra Jewels, always with a look of great intensity in his eyes. He is the author of more than 150 plays, many of which he also performed in and directed. At a recent symposium at the Judson Memorial Church centennial celebration, the Reverend Al Carmines recalled a letter from H. M. Kout-

H. M. Koutoukas soon after he arrived in Greenwich Village. Photo courtesy of Countess Olivera Savkovic.

oukas in which the playwright demanded that the roles in his play be cast with attractive, romantic men who possessed the evil qualities of Renaissance poisoners.

At the Ridiculous Theatrical Company he has enjoyed a comeback similar to the return to the screen by Gloria Swanson as Norma Desmond in *Sunset Boulevard*. The noted Ridiculous characters Harry has played include Svengali in *Big Hotel* and Eartha in *Der Ring Gott Farblonjet*. He is currently creating a sensation opposite Everett Quinton and George Osterman, playing the evil Baron de Varville in Charles Ludlam's *Camille* with the Ridiculous Company.

The following interview took place on a recent afternoon at a restaurant called Arthur's on Greenwich Avenue and Charles Street, a longtime hangout that hasn't changed much since it was called Jean's Patio. Arthur's welcomes a gay clientele and is home to theatre people, as well as twelve-step programmers, who like to "problem-solve" hour after hour over coffee, ham, and eggs.

Robert Heide: Rather than talking right off about your illustrious theatrical career, why don't we talk a little about the rehearsal process for *Camille* with Everett Quinton as director. How did you prepare for your character as the Baron de Varville?

H. M. Koutoukas: The Baron de Varville is a marvelous character! Well, we began with the book—Everett is very attached to the Ludlam script. Ludlam highlighted things in the script that were meant to connect with our own period. It is Ludlam, I believe, who brought *Camille* out of obscurity. Zeffirelli tried to do it that same year and completely failed. What year was it? There was something about Ludlam's version that made people identify with this spectacular "boat" of a woman.

RH: Boat?

HMK: They called them "batons mouches" after the tour boats that went around Paris. The courtesans were referred to as "batons mouches." When Ludlam first did his play, it was as a great floral piece and it helped save the company at that juncture.

RH: It had a wonderful tour, too, didn't it?

HMK: Ludlam did world tours and now we're having the same kind of phenomenal response all over again…in a new way.

RH: The play does seem somehow to speak to today. There's something about…

HMK: Romance, death and evil…

RH: All of which we continue to deal with today. The lifestyles of the evil and infamous!

HMK: But isn't *Camille* really about the art of dying gracefully?

RH: Right. And we've been seeing a lot of that…the dying of our friend…I saw you at Ethyl Eichelberger's memorial…he used to perform miracles on your hair.

HMK: Indeed.

RH: He did it blue once.

HMK: My one direction to beauticians and hair-do people is to give me a style that will get me arrested.

RH: You yourself have actually been played by other actors. *Native* readers would be interested in your association with Harvey Feirstein. Could you tell the readers about that experience…what it was like to work with the author-actor of *Torch Song Trilogy*?

HMK: Well, he was a marvelous houseboy! He was my general organizational clutter coordinator—and a very sweet boy, but he had the very same dreams as his mother. Alas.

RH: He appeared as you in Christopher at Sheridan Squared, which you wrote?

HMK: Yes. But then Harvey asked me to do a play he wrote called *In Search of the Cobra Jewels*, which was a charming play about me which everyone seems to have forgotten about. Why don't they revive that?

RH: You appeared in the play?

HMK: Yes.

RH: That's a connection we've had over the years—Maria

Photo by James D. Gossage

Joe Cino, Eddie Barton (or Bhartonn), and H. M. Koutoukas at the Caffè Cino, 1966.

Montez, *Cobra Jewels*, and Charles Stanley. The "camp" sensibility seems to have originated at Caffè Cino, didn't it?

HMK: They seem now to be erasing the Cino from the lips of those that profited most by it.

RH: It's an Italian restaurant now, on Cornelia Street.

HMK: Joe would have liked that.

RH: And wasn't there a porno shop there too?

HMK: New York is a porno shop.

RH: That may be true. You are a very noted dramatist who has won Obie awards and such...

HMK: Awards are a way of shooting a person down, don't you think?

RH: Controlling you? Harnessing your energy? Anyway, let's talk about some of your own favorite works, some of the early theatrical endeavors. The play that comes to my mind is *Tidy Passions*.

HMK: That one was quite popular and it had a lot of wonderful people in it who were seminal types of people... they went out and struck their demon seeds everywhere—Charles Stanley, Lynn Johnson, Eddie Barton, Stanley Beige—people so incredibly brilliant they were never heard of again. But your first play, I suppose, is always the favorite.

RH: What was your first play?

HMK: *The Last Triangle*—it was about the last survivors of a nuclear experiment, and it had Virginia Woolf and Noel Coward as characters. It was done on a double-bill with a play called *Only a Countess May Dance When She's Crazy* starring Carol Griffith. It won the National Arts Club Award and then it was revived Off-Broadway by Barbara Wise at the Actor's Playhouse with Gretel Cummings. It was entitled *Two Camps by Koutoukas*.

RH: Those were marvelous. I will never forget Johnny Dodd's fantastic psychedelic lights.

HMK: Well, Johnny Dodd, it could be said, lit an age. And I think he's now about to light yet another age. There's a whole generation following in Johnny's footsteps, but they're very large footsteps. Hard to follow that kind of brilliance.

RH: You were influenced by Mira Rostova?

HMK: It was Madame Piscator, if you please, the great acting teacher who came out of Boleslavsky. She and Miss [Stella] Adler are the only two great teachers of acting, if you can live through them. They have a sense of understanding what you're doing. No one seems to be understanding anything in this age of hype, in an internal sense, and the internal life, which Richard Boleslavsky and Michael Chekhov and Stanislavsky focused on, seems to be codifying into some sort of hype now.

RH: Is the magic missing?

HMK: The true formula is usually missing. Part of it is in the search for it, i.e., The Truth. I guess once you find it you can become consumed by it but you try to keep flickering as long as you can. The great part is that we are dealing here with the mysteries of life. We must take these mysteries from life and

Photo by James D. Gossage

H. M. Koutoukas, composer Robert Cosmos Savage, and light man John P. Dodd at the Caffè Cino.

translate them through beauty into something reaches out to everyone...like a play or a painting. That's rather a run-on sentence, but it was Proust who said there were certain things that could only be described by run-on sentences.

RH: Well, you've always talked that way.

HMK: You mean psychic babble—I'm a Babble-on-ian!

RH: Let me ask you about your acting theory. You started your own infamous School for Gargoyles, where I was an early member.

HMK: I worked with people who were very talented but they were emotional exiles. No one wanted to work with them and they all had their own peculiar gifts—Mary Boylan, Ethyl Eichelberger, Harvey Fierstein, Lisa Persky—who went on to star in movies like *Cotton Club*—and wonderful people dropped in on it too like Yoko Ono and those mischievous elves Gerry Ragni and Jim Rado.

RH: Every time I run into Gerry in the Village he's desperately looking for you.

HMK: Yes, we met and we did plays together. We never bothered very much with theories. You get into theories and you become like those overly moralistic people who are tied to a bed and reading De Sade. Morality is incapacitating. In the theater it's action and more action, building a play. It's not easy.

RH: When we first met many years ago it was in a coffee shop on MacDougal Street. I remember how impressed I was that you were actually sitting there reading Sartre's *Being and Nothingness,* which I was attempting to read at the time

HMK: Copies of *Being and Nothingness* under the arm were necessary below Fourteenth Street in those desperate days.

RH: In the play you did with Lisa Persky, *Grandmother Is in the Strawberry Patch*, there was a particular scene where the ladies were covering a table with contact paper and one says to the other, "It's almost like real formica!" Which kind of described the theatre at the time, heading for the destitution of the plastics age.

HMK: Heading for the Xerox. There were actually people putting their heads into the Xerox at that period and making portraits of themselves.

RH: Did you ever work with Warhol? I know you had a friendship with Pope Ondine.

HMK: No, never with Andy, but he was always gracious to me. Ondine I think of as almost a childhood buddy, Ondine Von Gay. Yes, Ondine would stop by and visit, battle-scarred from the Warhol wars. I met Andy at many of the parties that the Shah gave, and no matter what they say about the Shah, he did give a delightful party. And it was Warhol who introduced me to the patrons who gave me Carnegie Hall for a Christmas present.

RH: You did a Christmas presentation there?

HMK: Yes. *Turtles Don't Dream.*

RH: The real mentors of Off-Off-Broadway that come to my mind are Al Carmines, Ellen Stewart—La Mama—and

Joe Cino. I know you've had relationships with all of them.

HMK: It's the other way, I think it's the other way—it's Caffè Cino, then the Judson, then Ellen Stewart. Cino was first.

RH: Right. I'd love to hear you talk about each of those places.

HMK: Cino—and La Stewart in her early days—needed plays, and worshipped dramatists and playwrights. Now we have more of a sponsor-type theater where they expect something in return. You are sponsored only to fulfill a grant. It's like pretender presenters. There were great patrons in that time, like Isabel Eberstadt, who did so much for Jack Smith, and there were other wonderful people who just wanted to help artists. Now it's different—of course the more different it gets, the more potential there is for things to remain the same. We definitely came out of a period where it was all for art—and none of us knew what it meant, which was part of the charm.

RH: There's a lot of hoopla now about turning down National Endowments.

HMK: I can't wait until the Endowment goes right down the drain. It will get rid of mediocrity. Mediocrity is God's greatest gift. We've found that out in 1990! Let's hope it doesn't stay that way. Look...ten percent goes to artists, the rest goes to sleazy middle management, landlords, and Con Edison. Everybody gets paid but the artist. If people can't hang up a painting without a foundation grant they shouldn't be gallery owners. The arts were much more exciting when individuals actually went to the artist's studio. Now the gallery vampires come between the artists and their wares in order to control the marketplace. It's all marketing now. Halston announced that people could no longer make dresses. They could, however, make great publicity. He was a great marketing artist. And as for these Broadway Babes—as I refer to the uptown writers—they are mostly marketing people themselves, and God help them (if there is a God for them, and I hope there is—I also hope that He is a vicious God). The hype they issue forth has very little to do with inner life. A lot of what they think they know should just be put into files and forgotten, like so much political rhetoric.

RH: At the Cino things were put on for practically nothing.

HMK: Yes, but never forget that "nothing" includes the blood of the poet, too. The less they give you the more of your blood they will ultimately use.

RH: Didn't Cino chase away the grant people?

HMK: Well, yes, but Judson in a funny way is the most heroic—they refused all grants. They felt that an arts organization dependent on any foundation would of necessity have to change for the worse. And the Cino, well, Joe never wanted to sign anything. He just wanted the plays done. Joe only wanted to be surrounded by art, beauty, and love.

RH: You mentioned Halston, but you're noted as a fashion person who enjoys living in great style. I think you had an influence on Hibiscus, Steven Varble, John Eric Broaddus, and some of the costume art people...

HMK: I was involved for many years with Charles James, a great fashion innovator. Charles taught me to have only contempt for marketing people. Now I feel a great deal of contempt for a great many things. How long has it been since you've seen an interesting outré person on the street? The exception is the homeless. They are the kings and queens of our time.

RH: Could you explain that a little further?

HMK: Well, these street people are the people of the future. The nomads. There have always been marginal people but these people are being sacrificed to the great golden calf. Actually the worst criminals are now the ones that are worrying about crime, like the real estate people, the co-op owners. People who have jobs and food usually don't go out on the street to stab people. We're getting what we deserve. It's a civilization where you have barbarians who are now standing at the gate. So now they're against subsidizing the artist: but every major corporation or syndicate in this country, oil for instance, is somehow subsidized.

RH: The other day we talked about the epidemic. You

Photo by James D. Gossage

Charles Stanley as Jean Harlow in "Tidy Passions" at the Caffè Cino, 1965: "Glamour is dead!"

said you've lost a great many friends.

HMK: Plagues come and plagues go; and plagues tell us something about the society in which we live. The amazing thing is that despite the government, and despite all of the voodoo economics going on, that there is a community of gay people caring about one another. If we left it up to our political leaders they'd be running through the streets with bells and shouting, "Come out!" and then, "You're dead!"

RH: Has anybody ever asked you to write a play on the subject of AIDS?

HMK: An artist's main concern is, "should I now take that next breath?" We're all worried about the next breath. Quinton has developed a quintessential school now.

RH: Quintonessentialism?

HMK: Quinton takes the most tragic thing...death and dying...in *Camille*...turns it inside out, strangles you with it, and then gets you breathing again with a choking laugh. Isn't that clearly what it's about? He works with mirrors. He's a slam actor. Slam dancing and also bull-fighting. It's dangerous to be on the stage with him. Of course, it is my duty to be as perverted as possible here on this earth. You have to be alert when you're on the stage with him. You must focus and concentrate or your life's in danger. He makes incredible demands.

RH: Can you describe a demand from Everett?

HMK: He forces you to think rigidly about timing and holding and setting things from performance to performance. Quinton himself, of course, began as sort of a Cinderella at the Ridiculous and worked his bones off.

RH: What are the other characters specifically that you created at the Ridiculous?

HMK: I did the Mother of the Son in *Enchanted Pig*. Ludlam directed me in that. Ludlam created exquisite tortures for me but I wasn't able to enjoy them then. Then I did *Big Hotel* and *When Queens Collide, or Conquest of the Universe, Der Ring Gott Farblonjet,* and the present revival of *Camille*.

RH: Did you ever work with John Vaccaro? Didn't he originate the concept for the "Theater of the Ridiculous"?

HMK: No, I met him once or twice. Cino actually fired him from my play *With Creatures Make My Way*, which was commissioned to open at the Caffè Cino.

RH: Warren Finnerty was superb in that. I saw that.

HMK: Robert Sklar directed it. What ever happened to Roberta Sklar? If any of your readers knows where Roberta Sklar is, send her back to the theatre...into my life. I need her.

RH: I'd like to hear more about your plays.

HMK: They're camps—I call them camps. Plays are things of the Fifties.

RH: Your camps then. Would you care to name some of them?

HMK: *Invocations; Tidy Passions; Pomegranada,* an opera I did with Al Carmines at Judson, which was recorded. It's quite lovely, although now it is totally forgotten. Then there was *Medea in the Laundromat,* played by both Linda Eskenas and Charles Stanley; *The Machine That Couldn't; Black and Blue and Freezer Burned on Monday,* which was done at Lincoln Center. Let's see—there are so many. I've written over 150.

RH: You don't have to name them all. Readers can go to the Lincoln Center Library where they have the Cino files—files galore on "the quintessential Cino playwright." Isn't that what you've been called?

HMK: I'm not too interested in being remembered—or remembering myself. One of my goals now is to forget myself. Every day I try to forget and let something else enter into my consciousness.

RH: Younger people come to me—and I know they come to you—to ask about the sixties, and the Off-Off-Broadway theater. They want answers as to why, in their mind, it was so fantastic—or they want advice as to how to proceed in the theater today. What kind of advice would you give the young person starting out in a kind of artistic or creative career? I don't mean the commercial theatre.

HMK: Well, the first thing I would offer anyone would be my sympathy. The second is that if there is anything else they can do they should go do it. Cultural organizations, arts organizations, are now really telling young people what they must do. One of the goals is not knowing what we're doing.

RH: Should people draw their inspiration from outside of the theater?

HMK: Yes, they should refuse to draw inspiration from theater, film, or even the radio—with the exception of Kate Smith. They should draw from life. It is from office temp jobs that they will get the characters to write about. They should read. Proust. There may come a day when Proust will be the one to help them out of a terrible jam.

RH: Or Sartre? You live on Christopher Street. Have you noticed changes on Christopher Street in the last year?

HMK: Now it's very different when you live on Christopher Street, because it's your home, but it is a street that shows all the worst and all the good things of any period, as it always has. During the '60s, the boys were pretty, the drugs were good, and the tie-dyes were fresh. Then there was the moment of the revolution.

RH: Stonewall?

HMK: Yes, that was an error on the part of the tactical police.

RH: The Village keeps historicizing itself. I know Ross Wetzsteon of the *Village Voice* is writing right now a major history book on Greenwich Village and he'll be writing about you and he'll be writing about the Cino—in other words, he is now historicizing what they used to call the "new bohemia" of the '60s.

HMK: There are cycles, I'm sad and old enough to admit.

RH: When you write do you often think in very visual terms? Your language is very poetic…so visual in its impact.

HMK: Yes, I'm very inspired by painting and music, but I work from specific characters connected to situations they fall into. I do have some beginnings, middles, and ends, but I hope the day will come when we don't need them. The beginnings and ends, that is. I come out of a very deterministic type of journalistic writing. I went to the opposite extreme, you see. I learned how to diagram sentences when I saw a mobile and I thought diagraming sentences was like making a mobile.

RH: What do you think about gay life…where is it heading today in the '90s?

HMK: Gay is a lot more than a good party. My main concern now is what is going to get me through the day without my having to hate everything.

RH: So you wake up and you feel…

HMK: I've become cynical. But cynicism gives you pro-

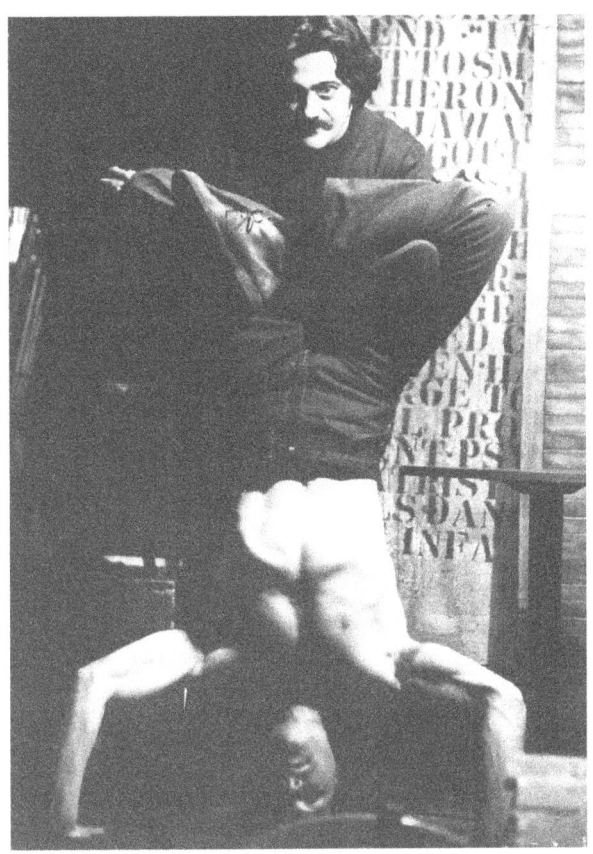

Photo by Eugenia Louis

H. M. Koutoukas with Jeff Weiss during production of "When Clowns Play Hamlet" at La Mama, 1967.

nounced cheekbones, they say. How can I continue—absorb all this pain and bitterness? How am I going to remain independent, free, and joyous? How am I going to make my tears glitter and turn them into something that gives someone some spiritual bullets to protect themselves with? And by spiritual I don't mean religion, although religion is a wonderful thing. I'm a member of the Judson Church. I dropped the church of my birth because I don't want to belong to a church that wants to burn me at the stake.

RH: I always like to ask about heroes in an interview—Greta Garbo, John Wayne. Who are your favorites?

HMK: Geraldine Page. Montgomery Clift. I've known them well.

RH: Monty had an affair with someone we know, who should remain nameless.

HMK: He made a great breakthrough. Monty took chances. He was open. Everyone who met him knew they were in the presence of someone great. That's why they now have to drag him through the mud. I like Wendy Hiller, Dirk Bogarde, people like that. I go to the movies to be charmed. And by the way, I don't believe talkies really have a great future. There are some wonderful stage actors: Jeff Weiss and Ethyl Eichelberger. I admire them.

RH: You worked with Jeff. He was in your play *When Clowns Play Hamlet.*

HMK: His very first debut.

RH: I think Jeff is a great actor.

HMK: They threw away the cookie-cutter for actors when they made Jeff. And there are also wonderful clowns like Ragni and Rado, the *Hair* boys. I also don't understand why actors like Roberts Blossom aren't put in temples where we can just go and watch them walk across a room. Then there's John Heys and Agusto Machado who are two greats. Why don't the headhunters come downtown and drag those two off? John Heys as Diana Vreeland was brilliant. Agusto does things our grandchildren—if we had any—should be taken to see. There are wonderful talented people right in front of us. Part of our duty is to recognize these people and see that they get a peanut butter and jelly sandwich. Forget grants.

RH: That reminds me of the times that we used to hang out at Mother Hubbard's and Clara's Pam Pam on Sheridan Square. They fed you there when you were a starving Village writer.

HMK: They would allow me to run up these incredible bills. And I wrote plays in the restroom. There was a preciousness, a sacredness to the artist to the restaurateurs in the '60s.

It's very hard to understand when you're living in a shoebox and paying $1000 per month rent. Young people today have embraced a new martyrdom. Theater is now just something to pass the time until they become one of those people who torch their wives and children in New Jersey.

RH: You've been called a playwright-as-poet, a poetic playwright, and also at Lincoln Center, at the anniversary ceremony honoring the Cino.

HMK: They tried to bury us alive there!

RH: You were called the quintessential Cino playwright. What does that mean?

HMK: Cino would call you up and say he needed a play. I would sit down at the typewriter...and give him a play. That's all.

RH: Are you working on a new play now?

HMK: I'm working on a play called *Athalia—Queen of the Jews* for Everett to be done at the Theater of the Ridiculous. It's just another theatrical device. I'm also working on a piece called *Nellie Twelve-Step* about a lady without a personality who gets involved in all the twelve-step programs at the same time and she's never heard from again.

RH: Like Rage-aholics Anonymous?

HMK: Well, I've heard there is a now a laundry anonymous for people who are obsessed with clean laundry. I see *Nellie Twelve-Step* as a little musical and *Athalia—Queen of the Jews* as a great epic tragedy. I've promised Everett a costume change for every entrance and I think he will have about twenty entrances. There will be a huge cast...

RH: I like the idea for your twelve-steps play. Does the Nellie refer to Nellie Vivas?

HMK: The Twelve-Step thing is for people who need it. Whatever helps you through the terrible night. If e.s.t. helps, bravo e.s.t.; if Scientology helps, then okay, sail away with Ron Hubbard.

RH: Anything that helps you get personal insight...

HMK: Well, I think we can all use a little insight. I know that I'll never get well and that I chose perversion over neurosis years ago. Freud gives us that choice, you know.

RH: Were you ever in analysis, Harry?

HMK: Darling, my life is analysis. And all of the analysts improved greatly working with me.

RH: Were your doctors of any particular school, existential or—

HMK: Freudian, Slavanian, and Aquatic Chimpanzee. The latter was the most charming of my many analysts.

RH: A lot of artists avoid psychoanalysis like the plague.

HMK: I don't think an artist should avoid anything. Remember, it was analysis that opened up a lot of people such as James Joyce. Even Trotsky was fascinated by Freud's writing. Freud should be read if only for his writing style. Diane Arbus and I used to sit around and read his case histories.

RH: And those of Wilhelm Steckel?

HMK: He knew his wines, they say.

RH: *The Patterns of Psycho-Sexual Infantilism* was one of Steckel's theses.

HMK: And Wilhelm Reich.

RH: Right. Does the idea of a crime wave in the Village scare you in any way?

HMK: No, because I'm an artist. As an artist I always take the criminal's side.

RH: Now we have the Pink Panthers on Christopher Street.

HMK: I worry about these young vigilantes because one construction worker from New Jersey with a lead pipe could…

RH: Knock them for a loop?

HMK: But if we call all our problems crimes we are simplifying and putting ourselves in danger. The ideal thing, the Christ-like thing, would be to take the mugger to coffee and… find those points where we connect with them. New York has always been violent.

RH: Yeah, weren't there the Hudson Dusters during Eugene O'Neill's time? A gang of wild Irish ruffians from down below Hudson Street.

HMK: Charming in today's context. When we look at

the criminal cities, New York is down somewhat on the list. I don't know if law and order is the answer, or more cops.

RH: Let's regress a little bit, since we didn't start out with any of your early life, where you grew up…

HMK: Well, I don't want to give my hometown any credit at all.

RH: Wasn't it Buffalo?

HMK: No, no, I don't want to even mention the name.

RH: Didn't another playwright grow up in the same town as you?

HMK: Nearby, nearby. I'm basically a Greek, you see. Let's not mention anything except the fact that I arrived in the Village.

RH: Where you invented yourself.

HMK: Yes, I come from very down-to-earth people. I have a wonderful aunt and a sister—here's their picture.

RH: Oh, charming.

HMK: She can never remember what my favorite pie is when I go home so the window sill always has five different fruit pies on it.

RH: What is your favorite pie?

HMK: Rhubarb.

RH: Not strawberry-rhubarb?

HMK: Rhubarb, just plain old rhubarb. I like the bitterness of it.

In Search of H. M. Koutoukas
by Donald L. Brooks

Prosaic recitation of the wit, antics, and inanity of the world of H. M. Koutoukas is easy; it is a tough task to look beyond and find his soul. In the process, I may speak of myself as much as my subject, but this is intentional, as I write about not just an individual, but my relationship with that individual. So, with trepidation, I sift through a lost sea of fifty years of memorabilia for H. M. Koutoukas—Harry as we knew him. The initials "H. M." always seemed to portend the mysterious, perhaps His Majesty, at the least, nothing as disturbing as Haralambos Monroe. One on one, he was "Harry," and in our little underground world of theatre, "Koutoukas." Searching through files for scripts and photographs, I find it difficult to capture his essence, elusive of all that is tactile and existing only in memory. Harry is gone and has taken with him H. M. Koutoukas, that brilliant creation I loved for half a century.

A poet first and then a dramatist in the mode of Federico García Lorca, Koutoukas was an irresistible figure whether through his actors on stage, the written page, the spoken word, or the silence that often cloaked a gold mine of prose waiting for the right explosive to dislodge an etymological effusion of glittering treasure. He was the wordsmith wonder of the underground in the days of the Caffè Cino, and along with so many other and varied artists traded madness and magic for a few nights of glory in an illegal bistro in the then-forgotten Greenwich Village of New York City. Make no mistake about it, this was an underground in every sense of the word, notwithstanding how tame it may now seem compared to the present-day riot of rot and excess of ego.

Working across town at Café La Mama, where Ellen Stewart and I sat in an empty loft closed the previous night for code violations, I found that sometimes the task of directing a

Photo courtesy of Donald L. Brooks
H. M. Koutoukas in "In Search of the Cobra Jewels."

play included giving a pep talk to the theatre owner, rebuilding the doors and exits, securing pails of sand and fire extinguishers, not to mention escorting actors from the subway to the theatre as they feared for their safety on the streets of the Lower East Side. La Mama and the Caffè Cino were heterogeneous—the Cino had a more daring reputation, and it had H. M. Koutoukas. To make a long story et cetera, a March 1965 fire destroyed the interior of the Cino, and Ellen Stewart crowded the Cino's scheduled productions into La Mama, whereupon two worlds became one for a few months of indiscriminate mingling.

I had seen Koutoukas productions of *Only a Countess May Dance When She's Crazy*, *With Creatures Make My Way*, *Pope Jean*, and *Pomegranada*. I requested that we meet, and it was arranged at La Mama. A handsome young man in his middle twenties, a few years older than me, appeared with a stuffed parrot on his shoulder, draped in a cape and surrounded by an entourage. The entourage was waved away as H. M. Koutoukas swept me off to 87 Christopher Street and a night of dreams I can't remember. Disappointed at being a mere curiosity of the flesh, uninterested in cocaine, overwhelmed by the disarray of the apartment's amassed material, which included three non-working refrigerators in the space of a small studio overrun with things that crawled, I gathered myself and my disappointment, greeting the bright light of morning alone with my fascination, nonetheless, intact. I was not the stone for sculpting a gargoyle to adorn the world of H. M. Koutoukas.

In the fall before Joe Cino's death, I returned from summer stock to find all my belongings discarded as garbage at the hands of La Mama's Paul Foster and 'Ntoni Bastiano. Everything. I was devastated. I was angry, expressed myself in pure heat of hatred, and was subsequently feared and unwelcome at the theatre I had built and nourished. I wandered. Having appeared in a benefit program for the reconstruction of the Caffè Cino at the Sullivan Street Playhouse (Bob Heide's *The Bed*) before I left for summer stock, I dropped in to take a look at the rebuilt café. Joe took me under his wing and put me to work doing lights, acting, repairs. I was to set and run lights that evening and had been waiting for the actors of a John Guare play to arrive. Harry hung out with Joe at the counter, eventually heading to the exit. In a misunderstanding, John Guare did not appear with his play and cast for a performance. I was in the light booth having just purchased and reading a Wonder Woman comic book ("The Secret of Tabu Mountain"). Upon hearing Joe Cino say, "What are we going to do, we have to have something," I showed him the comic book and said, "Let's do this!" Joe immediately brightened and sent Robert Patrick out for more copies at Lamston's five-and-dime two blocks away. I suggested that H. M. Koutoukas (who had just left the building) play Wonder Woman—he was chased down the street by Charles Stanley, brought back, given a headband, and a show went up on time. I changed the lights every time a comic frame occurred. By the end of the week, no one needed the script (comic book) but carried it anyway. It was the first comic book play at the Cino and the best. Others in the cast that night were Joe Cino, the suddenly present Johnny Dodd, Charles Stanley, and Deborah Lee. There was a great deal of satisfaction with that simple little fifteen-minute playlet, as I felt I had finally shared the muse with H. M. Koutoukas.

After Joe Cino's death, many of the artists never returned to the subsequently short-lived theatre/coffee house managed by Charles Stanley and others. Harry was reportedly in poor condition, having entered some sort of rehabilitation program at St. Vincent's Hospital. I recall that the major adjustment achieved in rehabilitation for Harry was the realization that he did not have to constantly entertain those around him—he became much more solemn and, of course, silent.

I had a successful play called *Xircus, the Private Life of Jesus Christ* completing a six-month run with a month or so still remaining on the lease of the Performing Garage in SoHo. The producer, Dick Briggs, was agreeable to a short run of whatever play I would like to mount. I contacted Harry and he gave me fragments of a piece called *Christopher at Sheridan Squared*, which was basically an uncollated pile of poetry. Many of the actors from *Xircus* would be in the production; however, I sent out word to Christopher Street that casting was being held. A good many actors in the production were not actors until they were cast in the play. Harry would send bits and pieces of writing from time to time during rehearsals and I fashioned them all into a narrative—it became a small epic of city apartment and street life. Harvey Fierstein, who had played Our Lady of 42nd Street in *Xircus* played what could be termed as the Koutoukas role. Music was on a harpsichord, composed by A. M.

Photo courtesy of Donald L. Brooks
"In Search of the Cobra Jewels," with Joe Salata (left) and Jon Robin Dewey.

Fine, a heterophobic and paranoid musical genius. A chorus of sorts chanted the lines and danced to choreography by James Waring. A full two-story set was constructed with a tapestry from the Metropolitan Opera as the act curtain. It was a wonderful piece with a full house on opening night and no audience thereafter. Harry was fond of one-night-only theatre stands—most of his plays could be seen but once. The second night, Harry positioned himself on the top tier of the wooden structure at the Performing Garage and threatened to hurl himself to the floor. I advised him that if suicide were intended that he might not succeed, merely crippling himself for life, paralyzed and unable to ever again attempt to terminate his existence.

Somewhere in my files is a script of our collaboration and an audio tape of a performance—the negatives for the photographs were maintained by Harvey Fierstein, leaving only a contact sheet of same. Fierstein was a demanding diva buttressed only by his being aware of his lack of experience. I recognized his wit and originality in his everyday conversations as being far more interesting than most of the plays that I was given to consider directing. I told him that if he would write a play, I'd produce it. This was twofold in purpose, it would shut him up for a while and maybe produce a lively theatre piece. He returned much too soon with a short play called *The Very Last Camp*—with Ellen and myself as characters. No. I was not going to do a play with a second-hand account of my relationship with forces I wanted to forget, and had no desire to provoke—Harvey had in mind another *Superfreak*, a play about the Caffè Cino that upset too many individuals in the Off-Off-Broadway scene. I sent him back to the proverbial drawing board with an assignment: clean H. M. Koutoukas's apartment!

Harry's apartment had become unlivable. It is reported that he dabbed glow-in-the-dark paint on the back of cockroaches so that one might turn out the lights and watch the spectacle! He needed to get it straightened so that he could at least find a comfortable corner for sleeping. I sent Fierstein and Russell Krum to do the chore, advising Harvey that if he searched deep enough into the experience, that a real play would be there, one that he could write honestly about. Well, he did. What was his and what was Harry's one will never know—the play was called *In Search of the Cobra Jewels*.

I approached Harry by chance on Christopher Street, a half-block from his apartment at 87, advised him that Harvey had written a play about him, but that I could not do it unless Harry would play himself. He responded, "Get me a script and a nurse for all the rehearsals and performances." I set a street actor, Flash Storm, to the task. He made sure that Harry was at the required rehearsals and saw to many of Harry's other needs during the time. Fierstein and I recruited Harvey and Ronald Tavel, Agosto Machado, and Mario Montez for an all-male cast including drag queens Alexis De Lago and Wilhelmina Ross, the stained-glass artist Gilly Glass, who played a window, and many of the street actors from *Christopher at Sheridan Squared*.

Opening night, near the conclusion of the first act during a chorale, Harry produced a razor blade and began marking his wrists, producing blood. Michael Smith, the *Village Voice* critic and a friend of Harry, was in attendance and noted in a review: *During the first-act finale of "In Search of the Cobra Jewels" last Wednesday, H. M. Koutoukas, who plays the central role, cut himself delicately and deliberately with a razor blade, just deeply enough so blood oozed out on his arms and face. Harvey Fierstein's play is transparently about Koutoukas himself in the form of Noel Swann, poet and playwright in flirtation with Death. And it is, further, a direct rip-off of Koutoukas's distinctive style as a dramatist—aphoristic, euphuistic, picturesque, tormentedly romantic, sentimentally nostalgic. But the opening night blood-letting introduced too much reality onto the stage for my taste. I was sickened and horrified. Koutoukas's gesture, though reviving an ancient sacrificial mode of theatre, by its very truthfulness seemed to go beyond art and call art worthless, and it had the effect of nearly destroying the play... Once again Donald L. Brooks has done a production that gets to me so personally that I can hardly talk about it coherently. Once again he has concocted an indecipherable mixture of brilliance, ineptitude, and nearly pathological acting out... Brooks certainly has a flair for raw theatricality, and he persistently confronts in his work subjects, styles, and personal equations which to others appear in bad taste and simply too dangerous. First I was entertained, then I was frightened, then I didn't know where I was and my mind was left burning with contradictions. What kind of theatre is that?* Well, it wasn't the kind I had intended, but Harry took care of that!

I went downstairs to the dressing room, where the actors

Photo courtesy of Donald L. Brooks

"In Search of the Cobra Jewels."

were a bit confused to say the least. Harry had just fled the theatre, and I went in pursuit, catching up to him about two blocks away. I chided him for such cheap theatrics, citing selfishness to the other actors, commanding him to return to the theatre to finish the performance, and further advised that he was going to do the entire schedule of performances and that if he decided to slit his wrists every night he'd be hamburger by the end of the run—also, to advise me beforehand of same so that I could make sure the audience noticed, as being that the lighting was in red, we were wasting the blood—a white light would show the deed more effectively. Well, he returned and there was no problem after that—he was perfect as himself in the guise of Noel Swann, speaking what surely were many of his own words plucked from the debris of his lair. Only Harry and his neophyte gargoyle could possibly know who wrote what and who played who.

Without a doubt, the best line to come out of Off-Off-Broadway was Harry's, utilizing an expletive that at the time was wont to make a censor swoon—at the end of the play, a lonely and ruined actress asks the audience, "Anybody want to fuck a star?!" Broadway never called, but Times Square occasionally drew Harry to its dark recesses, for I vividly recollect that while I was stripping at a seedy male burlesque house, his incongruous presence surprised me, along with our producer Dick Briggs, in the front row of the audience—caught in the act, indeed! The three of us attended a performance of Crowbar at the Victory Theatre on 42nd Street while it was still haunted from the ghosts of the early century. The Victory was the movie house that premiered *Ilsa, She Wolf of the SS,* a film with Koutoukas's participation toward the end of its use as a movie house—so he did get uptown once in a while!

The relationship never changed; every meeting was as though the last were the day before. We religiously exchanged Christmas cards for a quarter-century, and I always looked forward to seeing him on Halloween at Theatre for the New City, where he appeared as a celebrity judge for the costume parade at the Halloween Ball—his category was always the least conventional. When friends were dropping like flies from the plague, I told him that I had ceased going to anyone's memorial that I had not known for at least twenty-five years—he wrote that down too! I last saw Harry at the Obies at a hall at New York University, where he, Robert Dahdah, and I sat together in the lobby for a good half-hour while various individuals, including some of Harry's gargoyles, stopped by to pay their respects to the old men of the underground.

Now he's left us behind. Let us hope it is just another avant-garde movement and his beautiful soul is merely leading the way to where artists need not struggle against the oppressive forces of our world, but simply wave a hand and the imagination becomes reality. As we sift through his life, let us remember that while he lived, we many times stood aside while he destroyed his own creations. If the art of his muse that now lies scattered among the ashes can rise as the Phoenix into the light of a deserved appreciation alongside the great poets and playwrights of our time, then and only then will we ever have satisfaction and peace in search of H. M. Koutoukas.

We Were So Young Once
For Kenneth Burgess

Following rainbows to their very end
Fearless of the dark
Knowing of the protection of candlelight
In small red votive cups
Guided by our wit, led on by our charms
And the bright twinkle of bluebells in summer
Snowbells in winter
Church bells on Sundays.
Following rainbows that lead to the hearts
Of marble Adoni
Who guarded fountains
Of coloured water that caught tiny rainbow arches
Marble curlicue fountains
That hold penny wishes
O the penny wishes
And the dollar dreams
How many came true
How many forgotten.

No fear of the night
As long as there are candles
No fear of the day as long as
Laughter healed.
We were so young once.

—H. M. Koutoukas

27 November 1989

The Importance of Being Harry
by Penny Arcade

In the early hours of Saturday March 7th 2010 the restless spirit of Harry Koutoukas was stilled. I am sure I am not alone in wondering what Harry's last thought was. Few in the history of the spoken word were as salient as Koutoukas in summing up a situation in one enlightening, transforming and hysterically funny sentence. Yes, Harry was a wit. A real one. Like Oscar Wilde, Quentin Crisp, and Dorothy Parker. It was, I might add, his life's work.

Harralambos Monroe Koutoukas was born a twin in 1937 in Endicott, New York, into a Greek Orthodox family residing in that backwater shoe town. "Yes," Koutoukas mused, "I suppose if I had stayed up there in Endicott, I would have been a foreman in the shoe factory by now." Stay there he did not. Prescient even at age nine, with his own local radio program, "Talking Leaves," Harry met the drag queen, female impersonator, macrobiotic devotee, and 19th-century song specialist Minette in one of the local saloons that had entertainment while he was still a teenager, on one of the regional tours that Minette still engaged in through the 1940s and 1950s, when female impersonation was still an art form that minced through the rural towns of America.

While Harry's twin brother Paul would enter the Greek Orthodox novitiate, studying in Athens for five years, Harry would enter the sybarite Mystery School of post-World War II New York bohemia. Paul would become a bishop in the Greek Orthodox Church, an archmandrite, the highest order a celibate Greek Orthodox priest can attain. Harry was tremendously proud of his brother and often bragged about him. Paul would predecease Harry by less than two years, felled by the same diabetes that ended Harry's life.

Harry would become the Pope of Greenwich Village

even as he was highly identified with the East Village, doing many of his plays, which he called "camps," at Theater for the New City and La Mama.

Like the poet Max Bodenheim, whose presence remained alive for decades after his death in the telling and retelling of his legend, so it will be for Harry Koutoukas in the decades to come, because everyone who ever met Harry Koutoukas has a story to tell and one or more aphorisms and one-liners to go with it.

"Harry was vivid, confrontational, shocking, outrageous, and verbal—everything that is missing in today's theatre." said one admirer. "Harry lived in a fantasy world of being a highly successful, rich, and glamorous star, and this attitude attracted lovers, patrons, and fans," recalled playwright Robert Patrick in a recent phone call, "Most of us were gay and working class and we fled from our families and the passivity and mediocrity of the towns we were from and we all had that in common. We really never talked much about our backgrounds back then."

After Harry's death people wandered around in shock, many saying that they didn't know what they would do without Harry in the streets of Greenwich Village. But as Luc Santé pointed out in his brilliant book *Low Life*, "New York has never had any truck with its dead so they continue to wander the streets." Harry Koutoukas will never go away from the streets of downtown New York that he loved. Like Whitman, Poe, Ginsberg, and all the great poets, he walks the streets now and always will.

As H. M. Koutoukas wrote in his play *Awful People Are Coming Over So We Must Be Pretending to Be Hard at Work and Hope They Will Go Away*, "The night says things we aren't ready to hear, and only poets and the living dead may roam the night without fear."

H. M. Koutoukas: A Remembrance
by Lisa Jane Persky

My (four) parents moved to Greenwich Village because it was a different kind of place, with all kinds of people. People who were made to feel "different" or who actually were could be comfortable being themselves. It was still a place where differences were celebrated, reveled in—together. The children of Villagers took this for granted and expected the whole world would catch up pretty soon. If that meant homogenizing in the "melting pot" of New York that would be okay, too. Fun City. This was before New York was yoked with the nickname of the Big Apple, which any way you look at it is all about moolah.

It's impossible to bring the range, breadth, and scope of Harry Koutoukas or the Village of the 1960s and 70s into focus in a few words or pages, but in 1959 Harry moved to that Greenwich Village. That Greenwich Village, one of acceptance, promise and hope, exploration and artistic experimentation, lived on in Harry until his death.

Harry lived and died at 87 Christopher Street in Apartment No. 9. During his time there, I lived in the building both with my family and (later) without. I was eleven when we moved in and twenty-one when I left for Los Angeles. I got to know Harry from the privileged perspective of childhood.

Very early in our residency, Harry told me that the electricity in his apartment was generated by albino cockroaches who took turns running on a wheel in his bathtub.

If he didn't actually have the roaches mesmerized, he had me.

His mailbox bore a single name: Diana Prince (the actual identity of Wonder Woman). If undesirable mail or bills addressed to Harry somehow managed to get through, he would leave them unopened, mark them with an inked rubber stamp that read **DECEASED**, and drop them back into the mail.

Photo by Andy Zax

Harry Koutoukas and Lisa Jane Persky.

An elderly Italian lady, Rosie, and her middle-aged daughter, who also lived in the building, would stand in the doorway and people-watch on warm afternoons. Rosie loved the street show, but she couldn't rectify her devout Catholicism with her love of Village characters or her special fondness for Harry. Rosie explained to him that he shouldn't worry. He wasn't a homosexual. "You're just refined," she said.

"Yes, dear," he'd say with genuine affection.

Harry stayed out late into the night and would often be writing during the afternoons. He liked to wear outfits he called cos-*tumes*. Everything was theatre to Harry, it was his "normal," and that exaggerated approach to life itself translated well through him and his work. He moved with a unique kind of fluidity, which he once described to my mother as being "like the inside of a washing machine." Swooping was so much more interesting and fun than rounding a corner or picking up a bag of groceries in the usual fashion. Harry's huge protruding eyes and active brows made his expression one of constant awe, and surprise. Those eyes didn't land on much, they cased everything around him—even if you were sitting across from him engaged in a quiet conversation. Still, he was taking it all in, he heard you and it was all being absorbed for later, to be written into a poem or one of his "camps." His exotic style could be imitated, but not with the intelligence, wit, and force of his personality. This sometimes made him hard to please, and people had extreme experiences and trying times working with him on his plays. His restless search for perfection of character in life, writing, performance wasn't all style, it came from an exceptional scholarly man.

Even though Harry was highly educated, a philosopher-playwright, he wouldn't quite allow anyone to take him completely seriously. Doing so seemed to wreck his party. I knew I could never entertain him as well as his own mind was already doing. Still, for whatever reason, he indulged me with his time and gifts until his death. He was one of a very few people when I was young who made me feel as though I had some value as a person in the world.

Someone at his wake mentioned how he would take a word or a concept and change it around to make you completely rethink it, like "to live is to loathe," the original being "to live is to love" (Samuel Butler). All the ironies and contradictions were intentional and made him memorable to everyone. Everyone who knew him remembers things that he said. All told, it was not his attire, his body, or his words but his being in the world that was most exquisite and vivid. Truly, Harry was a gas.

In 1972, when portable video first captured the public's attention, Rudi Stern (of Electric Circus's Theatre of Light and Let There Be Neon) invested in the bulky equipment and started the Global Village collective—the idea being that video was going to unite us in the way that the internet finally has but with "heART." Harry wrote a script, a play for fire escapes called *Suicide Notations*. Some of us in the building were conscripted to play parts along with other cast members, and we took over the fire escapes on the front of our building for the day while Rudi and crew taped us. (I've tried to find out if this video still exists but to no avail. Stern died of cancer in the nineties.)

Later, when I graduated from high school (to no pomp and circumstance and no proud parents), Harry danced up to me on the street and said, "Darling, I've written a play for you. Rehearsal starts Sunday. The pay is twenty-five dollars a week. I'll send someone to pick you up." I was a cocky teenager with a ton of rage and energy, no focus of attention, and no real confidence of any kind. That Sunday, to my great surprise, Harry sent Benton Quin, the man who was to play Eunice, "the woman next door," to my apartment. We walked across town together to La Mama E.T.C., and I played Cordelia Wells, "the world's most perfect teenager." The play was *Grandmother Is in the Strawberry Patch*. Grandmother was played silently from a rocking chair by one of Harry's favorite actresses, Mary Boylan. Harry directed.

On opening night, about a quarter of the way through the play, with critics in the audience, the actress playing my mother went up on her lines, and the rest of us struggled to throw lines and reminders to help her get back on track. After a minute or two of this fumbling, Harry came lunging onto the stage from the back row shouting, "This is professionalism? Go back. Go back and start again!" So we did.

Later that night, the actress who played my mother was fired and instantly replaced by Harry's psychotherapist. I never knew if she was really his psychotherapist or if that was part of the theatre. His casting methods were clearly of the Schwab's Drugstore variety. With Harry it was good to believe in the drama of everything, not to resist it. It always led to feeling/being present in the world, even if only by making you self-conscious, second-guess yourself, feel like fleeing. Experiencing all and everything was part of the process. After the *Village Voice* review came out he said, "Darling, I've given you a career. Go be an actress."

And for twenty-plus years I was an actress. I studied and I worked hard at it mostly because Harry told me to. He jump-

Photo by Phil Stiles

started a sense of purpose in me. Sometimes I even made a living at it—and other times I wanted to kick him in the ankles for diverting me from what I might have been. When I would credit and/or blame him for my career, he would raise his crazy eyebrows and say, "Dar-LING!" and laugh. I always think of Harry as one of my angels. When he came to see me when I appeared on Broadway or told me he was proud of me, that was my Oscar.

Six years after *Grandmother Is in the Strawberry Patch* I was in L.A. at the Whisky a Go-Go seeing Nico when I ran into

Tomata du Plenty (Cockettes, Screamers). He said, "I've been meaning to ask you something. I saw you at La Mama in *Grandmother Is in the Strawberry Patch*, and Harry Koutoukas charged the stage and made you all start over. Was that part of the play? Because that was grrrreat!"

Around that time Harry began calling the people he populated his plays with his "gargoyles" and told me I was one of the early graduates of the School for Gargoyles. It's the only degree I hold. In an uncharacteristic move that relieved many but surprised more, he also got a telephone. He made sure to tell me. "I'm in the book. Under B. A. Gargoyle."

Since then, I visited Harry year after year, every time I returned to New York. We enjoyed great and challenging times. We also always had closure. I saw him bitch but never complain, even when he lost a toe to diabetes.

In the last two years of his life, a number of people he felt deep kinship and connection to passed away. Two of them were tenants in the building on Christopher almost as long as he was. Another was his twin brother, once a bishop in the Greek Orthodox church. Harry seemed to fade. He was having more and more difficulty breathing and getting around, in spite of the donation of a motorized scooter by Yoko Ono, another former tenant of 87 Christopher Street. Dubbed the Glittermobile, it definitely gave him some extra mileage.

The last time I saw him, in September of 2009, was at his apartment. He was sitting on the side of his bed wearing a very chic and expensive robe. He lit his cigarette right next to his oxygen tank. I thought he was going to blow us to kingdom come right then, but you could never stop him from smoking, even when he was admitting to coughing up bits of lung.

In the spirit of his favorite author, Ouida, who said, "Christianity has made of death a terror which was unknown to the gay calmness of the Pagan," I thought, okay, I'm on board, this is part of being friends with Harry. Exploding would just have to be looked at as another great adventure we were on, the next, better play.

Harry took risks of all kinds, especially with himself.

Those who knew him well know that he had many opportunities to die over the years but did not choose them. When I spoke to him at the end of February 2010, he was tired, didn't like for people to have to help him up the stairs, was upset that he wasn't able to get out and about, said he didn't want the doctors to remove any more of his foot. This was as close as he ever got to complaining to me. He was still fiercely and fearlessly himself, and I believe he made a choice.

He asked Judson Church's Reverend Donna Schaper for the full Greek Eucharist upon his death. The Eucharist, in Greek Orthodoxy, is a metaphorical sacrifice for both the living and the dead. He stayed with the play until he finished the last act.

When the attendees sing Harry out with his own song, "The Rhinestone Crucifix," it won't be funereal, it will be coda.

To me, Harry's keen intelligence, his very particular faith and loving nature, sharp wit, exotic wardrobe, eccentric talent, and his many mysteries will always make him archangel, patron saint, mother/father of all true Greenwich Village denizens. He might well have hidden a pair of giant wings under that famous cape.

That last time we spoke, I asked him if there was anything I could do for him. He said, "Think good thoughts." I did and I will.

Thank you, Harry. Thank you.

An illustrated version of this article can be found on Lisa Jane Persky's blog, at http://noirpictures.blogspot.com.

Koutoukas Plays Binghamton
by Jan Quackenbush & Tim Gleason

Binghamton, New York, small as it is, contained by the Chenango River on one side, on the other the Susquehanna, has produced more than a few interesting characters in the world of entertainment and theatre, including Rod Serling, Leonard Melfi, and "His Majesty" H. M. Koutoukas. Harry is more accurately associated with his home town of Endicott, just up the river. Nevertheless, it was a Binghamton theatre company, the Know Theatre, started in 2002 by Tim Gleason, which brought Harry's astonishing work to Upstate audiences.

In 2003, Gleason produced *Awful People Are Coming Over So We Must Pretend to Be Hard at Work and Maybe They Will Go Away.* (The title is a phrase, says Gleason, which Yoko Ono once spoke to Harry at a party.) This was followed by *The Last Triangle* in 2004, *Quicksilver* in 2005, *A Letter from Colette* in 2006, and *Grandmother Is in the Strawberry Patch* in 2007.

Harry's plays were presented as part of Know Theatre's annual Playwrights and Artists Festival, which each fall featured a triple-bill of three established playwrights: H. M. Koutoukas, Leonard Melfi, and myself, Jan Quackenbush. Area artists (composers and painters) were invited to read the plays prior to production, select their playwright, and then render an art work based on impressions drawn from the script. Harry loved the idea and was very moved by the artworks based on his plays.

Harry—who traveled up from the city to see each of his plays—thrilled the audiences both in person and with his work. He was always stately and passionate as he answered questions in the talk-back sessions that followed the performance. He seemed uniquely wise, profound in his answers about theatre, the writing process, the hard work, labor, and life of a dramatist as he experienced it.

To say that Harry was gracious doesn't seem to say it "all"—better to leave that "all" to Harry. But he was gracious. He was magnificent. We love him, and will always remember him as "His Majesty."

To conclude this brief remembrance, here is Mr. Tim Gleason:

My first in-person meeting with Harry Koutoukas was a bit of a shock. He arrived for our symposium with green hair, a bearskin coat that reached to the floor, and a cane. But when he answered the first question, his love of theatre and writing eased all concern and made my life-long adoration begin.

From the first production on, I received Valentine's, Easter, and Christmas cards from him, always with words of encouragement. His "tide" lifted my theatre company to a new appreciation of the art form.

Every year an artist named Laurence Guidici religiously selected Harry's work and painted for him, every year of the Festival, awesome works!

We at Know Theatre are dedicating our 2010-2011 season to the memory of H. M. Koutoukas.

Obituary

Published in Binghamton Press & Sun-Bulletin, March 14, 2010

Harry M. Koutoukas, 72, passed away on Saturday, March 6, 2010, at his home in New York City. He is survived by his sister, Jean Ann Davidson of Endwell; a niece, Julie Davidson of Seattle, Washington; cousin, Susan Glickman and her spouse, Alan of Hurley, New York; and cousin, Victor DeWitt and his spouse, Mary Ann of Binghamton, New York. Mr. Koutoukas was predeceased by his parents, Harry P. and Agnes Koutoukas; and his brothers, The Very Reverend Paul Koutoukas and Robert Ogden.

Mr. Koutoukas was a graduate of Union-Endicott High School before moving to Manhattan in the late 1950's where he attended The New School. Harry went on to become an accomplished Actor and Playwright, earning numerous awards for his accomplishments. Harry was part of the Caffè Cino community as well La Mama ETC and the Theater for a New City, earning the name "Godfather of Off-Off Broadway." Harry was also very active in his beloved Judson Memorial Church in Greenwich Village. A memorial service will be held on Sunday, March 28, at 2:00 p.m. at Judson Memorial Church, Washington Square South, New York City.

H. M. Koutoukas
by Cookie Mueller

from *BOMB 5,* Spring 1983

H. M. Koutoukas writes and directs plays. Although there's been no full-scale public production in about four years, he's had 150 Equity-approved extravaganzas and 40 one-act pieces produced. Years ago, he had a workshop called the School for Gargoyles where such people as Harvey Fierstein, Gerome Ragni, James Rado, and Tom O'Horgan, among others, were the gargoyles who since have graduated into statues.

"I'm everybody's cheerleader," he says.

I went to his home late one afternoon for this interview; the candles in the overhead chandelier were burning and the place had that Gothic antediluvian look. I found Koutoukas and George Afamis, the handsome Cyprian, brewing coffee and reading. We laughed a lot throughout this interview. Koutoukas is very quick.

Cookie Mueller: Shall I ask you questions?

H. M. Koutoukas: Whatever you want.

CM: I do have a couple of questions. Is the white in your hair real?

HMK: Bleached. I decided to look the way I feel. Everyone thought I was dying my roots black. Some people get their blond hair by squeezing cats over their heads.

CM: I was thinking, the last time I saw you, you looked like Auntie Mame in mourning. You know, the sophisticated widow look. But I see now part of it is magenta.

HMK: This is my Christian hairdo. Santa's helper falls into the color Xerox machine. I'm working my way toward the Bride of Frankenstein look. Was that a question? Yes, my hair is real.

CM: This issue of BOMB...

HMK: Oh, I was the first dramatist to bomb a theatre where my play was showing.

CM: Yeah, oh yeah. What about that?

HMK: Well it was a play where the audience had a chance to leave with the cast or stay and hear the last monologue. The backers wanted it cut. They just came up to me, me, the writer, director, and maniac in charge, and said that this scene wouldn't be done. I said, "It's my play and I'm directing it and you're telling me I can't bomb the theatre?" And they said, "Well, it's rather expensive, Mr. Koutoukas. You need a new theatre each night." They had some sort of fear of the people in the audience with heart conditions. Why do people with heart conditions go to my plays instead of to the hospital? I just felt it was an important scene. It was gorgeous. Exquisite. Yellow smoke. New York audiences are the best. They stayed.

CM: When did you first start writing?

HMK: I always wrote. Suicide notes from the earliest age. They're my great specialty. I still couldn't get my parents' attention so I got a radio program...I was nine...national radio with a thing called *Talking Leaves*. It started as a little local thing.

CM: Where?

HMK: A little town called Endicott. It's upstate. 6000 people. A little shoe town.

CM: So when did you start writing plays?

HMK: I wrote my first play because it was either that or jump out a window. Ondine and Martin Proctor who owns Unicorn City both told me to send it to this contest and I did it as a joke. It was the National Arts Club Competition and there were all these heavy-duty writers. In a few months I was the recipient of the National Arts Award so I thought I had hold of a new thing here. It was better than writing bad checks. Although bad checks are the purest form of poetry.

CM: So you followed through on that talent?

HMK: Yes. People who don't do that are the people you can't help.

CM: That's the biggest sin, I feel, too.

Photo by James D. Gossage

Joe Cino and Harry Koutoukas at La Mama in 1965.

HMK: Yes, that and talking about art all night. When I started writing plays I couldn't stop. I wrote a play a day because I learned that one thing...you have to sit down and finish projects. It's the hardest thing to learn.

CM: Didn't you tell me you were writing a five-pound play?

HMK: Oh yeah. I'm also writing a thing called the *Afamis Notes* and *The Brown Book*. I try to find five things each day to write about. It's a bitch but I think it will teach me to write prose. I'm not aiming at a great work of fiction...I'm aiming to get one simple sentence after another.

CM: You never wrote prose?

HMK: No, the theatre is wonderful. Someone walks out on stage and puts the vase on the table. But when you write prose you have to write the vase, the enameling on the vase, the period of cloisonné. You have to write the shepherd and the shepherdess, and what they're wearing. Then you have to adjust each flower. It's brutal.

CM: I write prose. I find it difficult to write plays.

HMK: One doesn't write plays—they're written. You find the characters, then you get different hats, and the characters pace from room to room in different hats. It's much simpler.

You have to learn to listen to write plays. But since they fixed my radiator, I'm not hearing so many voices lately.

CM: Did you see *Eraserhead*?

HMK: No.

CM: It's all about people in radiators.

HMK: Would you like another light on you? Because I read in Ruth Draper that a yellow light cures anything.

CM: I wonder if that's true. Isn't yellow for paranoia?

HMK: I think they discovered that there's no such thing as paranoia. Now it's called heightened awareness.

CM: Do you know that thing about pink?

HMK: It's the navy blue of India.

CM: Putting people in pink rooms weakens their muscles.

HMK: Weakens their muscles? That explains it. I'm still trying to figure out what is fact. Because science gives us facts which are really like what old ladies told our mothers in laundromats.

CM: In all religions every color has a symbolic significance.

HMK: I stick to black. Black and blue. I'm getting to like the terrorist colors though.

CM: Once in a play you wrote, did you drop amphetamines from the balcony on the audience?

HMK: No, no…that was a play in which God gives up his personal stash of amphetamines because the Cobra Cult can't sleep…they die without cobra food. I had nothing, of course, to do with it. *[laughter]* But some dandies took the glitter and replaced it with amphetamines. We had several novels written about that play. The audience couldn't stop writing when they got home. Of course, in those days it was legal.

CM: When was this?

HMK: I'm not sure of the date. It was originally done at Carnegie Hall and there were several sleepless nights for the Carnegie Hall people who went to concerts because every time there was a high note some would come off the gilding. Are you in Peter Hujar's new book?

CM: No, but you are.

HMK: Here it is.

CM: I always feel uncomfortable in front of a still camera.

HMK: Well, cameras steal your soul. You get a feeling you're being hunted. It's like being analyzed. That's why Rilke would never get analyzed. He thought if they got rid of the demons the angels would go, too.

CM: Do you have any dates for your new play?

HMK: At the Theater for the New City, maybe. Valentine's dayish. But I have no dates. You don't begin dating until you're forty.

CM: You know the only play that I'm really familiar with of yours is *The Butterfly Encounter*. And it was really Greek to me. I don't mean that figuratively. I mean literally. The whole structure was like ancient Greek drama. For instance the chorus that talked to the actors and the audience.

HMK: In the beginning of my career I tried to write a play in each of the great styles of theater. I tried a restoration play in *Turtles Don't Dream*. I did a *Medea* which took place in a laundromat. The old Greek plays are like telegrams. You know...STOP! Jocasta's hung herself! STOP! My new play is called *Disarming Attachments*. I was going to write a little one-act nuclear freeze play but then I realized how the nuclear thing affected the family and what we are attached to. The things that would be broken. The things that are threatened that can't protect themselves. I realized it's not one act.

CM: You're really doing a lot of work.

HMK: I'm writing about "simple exchanges" and "terminal sex." People who want to die while having sex. This is quite a plague. Howard Smith promised me he'd do some research on it. But you know the *Village Voice*. They haven't been able to cut the mustard since...

CM: The '60s.

HMK: I don't know what's going on now. Do you? Life-wise?

CM: Sociologically?

HMK: The way we artists go, the rest of the world will go. The artist is always going 20 years before. We're not helpless, we're hopeless. Since the Second World War. All those people went to concentration camps looking for new jobs and showers. Is life more important than death? I'm Greek. I'll die for the publicity.

CM: I sort of believe that everyday you live past twenty is punishment. One should die young for painting or a cause or in a terrible trapeze accident. But now they've extended our life spans. But I'll never die. I'll just go on talking. [Koutoukas admitted to me earlier that he didn't reach true babblehood until he was twenty-five.] They'll put the artist's brains in tubes.

HMK: But, please bury me on a spit so every time there's a bad theatre production I'll turn automatically.

CM: The artists are now the technologists.

HMK: Yes, they go to their machines. One Con Edison blackout or an SS invasion and that art is gone. There is one reason why theatre goes on…you can even have theatre in concentration camps. Sartre talks about how when he was in a concentration camp…he was in a unit that did entertainment. There has always been theatre.

Did you know that the government in ancient Greece destroyed many of the plays that upset them—if the audience was made to weep for the enemy, for instance, or the play was slightly subversive. There's only the compromising ones left. Sophocles talks about many plays we've never seen.

CM: Who? Socrates?

HMK: No. Socrates was the child molester. Sophocles.

CM: I read somewhere that just in 1958 a play by Menander was dug up. I forget how to pronounce his name. Men…Mem…

HMK: Mamet? David Mamet was dug up? They should put him back in the jar.

CM: Tell me about your new play.

HMK: The play opens with this ruined Greek philosopher. Whenever he smiles his teeth are so bad that you see the Acropolis. He lives in a Greek take-out paper cup with the Acropolis on it. And then there's Malvina Falkland who has buck teeth: she throws them into the ocean so the penguins can escape to the Antarctic. She is in love with this ghetto type character; he's a vineyard owner and then Attila the Hun comes in wearing carrier-ship battle shoes and she dances with the five-headed general who always talks you to death. Then there's the boy who's just seen the abyss and can't get over it.

CM: What would you say about your style?

HMK: None of my plays are stylistically the same.

CM: You wrote plays for the Caffè Cino.

HMK: Everybody went through the Caffè Cino. They went through there because once this lawyer who wanted to do one of my plays on Broadway told me that life was a compromise so I pretended to go to the bathroom and left. I did the play at the Cino. Cino would come to playwrights and say, "Do you have a play for me this week?" There was a need for a different play each week, so you'd have a play ready.

CM: Would you compromise now?

HMK: I don't think I could.

CM: Well then you have to be your own backer.

HMK: You can become one of those maniacs that feel they have to do everything. I've always wanted to do a play like that; the audience comes in, you're selling the tickets, then you become the usher, and when the curtain goes up you're all the characters. During intermission you're selling popcorn.

CM: People always say you're self-destructive. Do you feel you are?

HMK: It's part of the show. My plays have always opened the day they're supposed to, always run their runs. But now, if mediocrity gets in the way... You remember in *Butterfly Encounter* they wanted to cut it. Well, what the hell am I in experimental theatre for? One of the reasons I've always stayed with experimental theatre is that you can write five-hour plays.

You can write about centipedes that live in sneakers and turn out to be madmen. I've lasted a long time to be considered a self-destructive person. But I don't know whether I'm destructive or not...I'm willing to listen to criticism.

CM: It's almost a proverb...great artists are self-destructive.

HMK: I'm worried about the young playwrights.

CM: Why?

HMK: Because there used to be a place where plays could be given a chance.

CM: Do you think there's a new style of writing?

HMK: I'm working on it. The great writers invented new ways of putting things down on paper. Emily Dickinson invented inner rhymes.

I just hope that our new writers can give us beautiful questions. While dying, Gertrude Stein was asked, "What's the answer to it all?" She just looked up and said, "What's the question?"

We're all going to end up swinging on that question mark.

Brief Comments

Yoko Ono

Harry and I met in a very strange situation. This was the sixties. I was living in the apartment next to his. I had a terrible argument with my then partner, who banged the door and left the apartment. Silence. Then I heard somebody knocking on my door very quietly. That was Harry. He invited me for tea at his apartment. He made tea, never mentioning what he obviously heard through the paper-thin wall. He was very considerate. I have never forgotten that afternoon—and how sweet Harry was.

James Rado

Harry was a great friend to Jerry (Ragni) & then, when I caught on, to me. When we walked along the street, or in the last few years, when late at night we sat in the cookie shop (Bleecker & Christopher), I would sometimes start writing down what he was saying. Some of my scribbles are impossible to decypher, but here are two readable ones:
  Live free & contented.
  Do not point! A lady should only point when in danger.

Jean-Claude van Itallie

How sad, Harry's passing. For decades my meetings with Harry on the streets of the Village have been accidental, occasional, cordial, and always a pleasure. We'd happily wave, recognizing each other as part of that dwindling fraternity of gay playwrights who were young in the Village in the sixties. We'd chat, glad to recapture for a moment the exciting past we shared. Harry was congenial and modest at these meetings though

Photo by Peter Hujar

happily I could always spot the invisible gaudy-feathered parrot on his shoulder. I shall miss meeting him. I wish him godspeed. His madcap antics were an antidote to a world gone mental.

Jim Gossage

After the Caffè Cino burned [in March 1965] I phoned or wrote, and Harry was the one who contacted me and asked if I would photograph the benefit being held at Writers Stage. I did. Not long after that Harry asked me to take some photos at a production he did at Coda Galleries, and over the next several years I saw and enjoyed many performances of plays by H. M. Koutoukas. Knowing that Harry has passed away reminds me even more strongly that Caffè Cino, Joe Cino, and too many others have left us also. Harry presented a fantastic image, with cape and a "stuffed" parakeet on his finger or lying on a chair or table with his hat. The way he put words together to present tenderness amid humor and chaos was also fantastic. I now feel a little cheated that I missed some of his productions.

Ann Harris

Harry made me a "gargoyle." I acted in three of his plays, and liked his directing style. Harry was considerate of his actors. He had us look for and remove nails, splinters, and staples from the stage because we were often barefoot. I remember running around town and having fun with Harry, Gerome Ragni, and Jim Rado when we were all doing a show at Lincoln Center—our own little gang. You felt like family with Harry.

Walter Harris

From the time the Harris family first landed in Off-Off-Broadway in the early 1960s, Harry was a constant presence, like a combination guardian angel and colorful uncle. I guess we all grew up together, including Harry and all the great Off-Off artists who were mostly in their twenties and thirties at that time.

I first got to know Harry during rehearsals for his operetta *Pomegranada*, co-written with composer Al Carmines and performed in the choir loft at Judson. Al and I were the orchestra. It was more from Harry's writing than from personal interaction that I came to understand him. Two of my favorite lines from his libretto are: "We choose our hell to save our grace" and "Why oh why has life become so sporty, so gamey? That we play Monopoly instead of constant ecstasy?"

Harry knew that I dabbled in 8mm home movies. He invited me to film a rehearsal of a show he was preparing at the Cino—I can't even remember the name. Halfway through I realized there was no film in the camera, or in my bag. Harry blew past his disappointment, smiled and whispered to me (out of earshot to the actors), "No matter—they're behaving. Keep rolling!" The actors continued brilliantly, as though they were on a Hollywood sound stage. I pretended the film was lost by the lab.

I last saw Harry recently in Seattle, where I live, during a visit with his niece. Though obviously having great physical difficulty (and smoking like a chimney), Harry entertained us in high style, as funny and jovial as ever. I was pleased to give him a copy of the Pomegranada score, lovingly and faithfully transcribed by David Tice from the cast recording, and promised him that I would make sure *Pomegranada* would one day enjoy a revival. And I will.

Marjorie Lipari

Harry, dear Harry... Bless your dynamic being.

My brother Victor, whom Harry joins in the hereafter now, is very present to me at this moment. He introduced me to Harry when I was young and overly tender of heart.

I remember being intimidated by him. But as time passed, Harry became so much gentler and always treated me with the utmost respect. I loved him and I will miss him.

Mel England

I met Harry in the Village sometime in the late nineties. He invited me to breakfast at Manatus and told me he was working on a play about penguins. I thought, this man is either completely insane or a genius. But I already knew it must be the latter, from listening to his wit over toast with marmalade. He was obviously the smartest, funniest and perhaps wisest person I'd ever known.

Harry was a regular at Manatus, and I regularly joined him there for breakfast, laughing loudly, non-stop, at his never-ending witticisms.

He knew I was an actor and always asked if I was making the "rounds." One morning I told him I'd been accepted to do a solo show in the New York Fringe Festival, showing him the contract and confessing I was terrified. It was perhaps the only time Harry was ever downright forceful with me. He said, "Darling, you MUST do this!" and he took a pen from his pocket, put it in my hand, and pushed my hand down to sign the contract.

I went to see his *Picture Perfect* at Theater for the New City. I was mesmerized. His play was sublime, deep, harrowing, and funny.

Not long after, he announced he'd written a part for me in his next play, *Ring of Death*. I was thrilled!

Early this spring, after a few years working in California, I was back in the city and called Harry to meet for our normal breakfast. He asked me to come by his apartment instead. It was now difficult for him to get up and down the stairs. So we had lunch. He had me order up tuna sandwiches from his sandwich shop.

I admired his pictures and memorabilia, proclamations honoring him, pictures of him performing in Camille in London, pictures of him with his many friends.

I said, "Harry, what an incredible life you've had!"

He looked at me, and with his trademark grandness, with all the drama he could muster, and tinged with his bittersweet ironic humor, he raised his eyebrows and pronounced. "It's all the PAST!"

A week later he was gone.

Maggie Low

I knew Harry through mutual friends in the Village. I learned bits of his life and work. He told me tales of happenings on the roof with Yoko, pre-John, studying with Piscator at the New School, and of course memories of the Caffè Cino.

In the early nineties I had the honor of becoming a Gar-

Photo by James D. Gossage

Harry Koutoukas, Paul Foster, and Ellen Stewart at a benefit for the Caffè Cino at Writer's Stage, March 1965.

goyle. I was walking down Perry Street and spotted Harry Koutoukas at the end of the block.

"Harry! How's the play going?" I knew he had a new one at La Mama.

"Dar-LING! You're in it!"

The leading lady had thrown a diva fit and walked out on opening night, and Harry had gone on in the role. He took my hand, led me to Manatus on Bleecker Street, and we read through the entire play together. It was Skin of the Night, about an Artichoke who falls in love with an Iris.

That night I went on with the book in my hand, playing Hortensia, "the Houseplant of Bernarda Alba." I often quote Harry's note on my acting: "Too much Hepburn, add whiskey!"

In 2004 he offered me a play to direct, The Ring of Death. I was convinced that he had started off with a character named Prudence, gotten up for coffee, come back and continued writing, only now calling her Patience. Stage directions were scarce. Harry was giving me a wonderful opportunity but I hadn't much experience as a director. So I asked him to join me at a back table at French Roast. I had put faces on old wooden clothes pins to represent each character, some wearing Equal packets, some Sweet 'n' Low, and we enacted the play among the sugar bowl and salt and pepper. Needless to say both Patience and Prudence remained in the play. We had a wonderful run at Theater for the New City.

Harry added so much to my life. He was a friend, teacher, and collaborator—the unofficial Mayor of Christopher Street.

Stephen Koch (director of the Peter Hujar Archive)

H. M. "Harry" Koutoukas, great flaming albeit almost forgotten flamingo of the theatrical madness that gave us Rado, Ragni, and Charles Ludlam, has died at 73. The theatre of painless outrage (apart from the ache of laughter) has lost the most reckless player of all.

Koutoukas spun out the kind of flamboyant throw-away drama that Hujar loved, and Hujar included Koutoukas among his elect: he's in *Portraits in Life and Death*. (Scholars' alert! Explain this: At the very last minute, Hujar dropped his wonderful portrait of Andy Warhol from the book. Why? "He's too famous.")

But the Koutoukas face? Peter never tired of it and had endless fun with it. But there was more. There may be more Hujar portraits of Koutoukas than Ludlum, or Paul Thek, or even David Wojnarowicz. If you can plumb the mystery of what Hujar saw in that mug, you'll be a master of theatre, and the art of portraiture, too.

Heather Rose Dominic

Harry, who always had time to offer/Lighting up rooms in which he stood/That time was always bright.

Robert Patrick

Harry was the great jokester, phrase-maker, and mythologist of the Cino. "Tacky glamour" was his coining. His *Turtles Don't Dream* played at Carnegie Hall, a tremendous slap in the face of the establishment. It was a play about the Cino as the temple of a "Cobra Cult." (One character told another, "Go and see if the temple supply of the sacred white amphetamine powder is running down. But hurry back—being alone ain't what it used to be.") Characteristically, he threw the play on so fast that it started with no final scene. Charles Stanley improvised a magnificent one. Charles also played Harry's mighty *Medea*.

Harry was often described as self-destructive or at best self-limiting. He would announce plays that never happened (the Cino schedule shows several of them), refer people who wanted to publish or produce his work professionally to an unlocatable and possibly nonexistent Swiss agent, and is the subject of several legends about fantastic brawls and brannigans, one involving him throwing a famed Off-Off producer down a flight of stairs. He encouraged such stories.

He loved the Cino and Off-Off, perhaps the only place he could ever be accepted uncritically. As Off-Off expanded, he sarcastically said he was going to make a fortune with a bus that would take tourists from the 7 o'clock show at the Cino to the 8 o'clock at La Mama, the 9 o'clock at Judson Church, the 10 o'clock at Theatre Genesis. However, he produced at all of the early theatres, including a version of *Salome* privately subtitled *Give Head* and a vampire play called *He Sucks*.

Harry played Wonder Woman in the rapidly improvised

first Cino comic-book play. As time went on, his appearance varied more and more kaleidoscopically, with Krazy Kolors, mohawks, and such. He was protected in his later years by Jimmy Rado and Yoko Ono, among others.

My favorite memory of Harry is from the day I took him to see the delirious Maria Montez movie *Cobra Woman* for the first time. Incredibly, he had co-opted it and incorporated references to it into his work without ever having actually seen it. He was very excited as we sat in the seats of Theatre 80. When the screen lit up with a gorgeous lagoon, he clutched my forearm and cried, "Ooooo, is that a set or a costume?"

Rest in peace, dear poet.

Bob Shields

Good grief!

Harry appears before God who tells him, "You seem to have led a pretty wild life. I still can't make up my mind what to do with you."

H. M. replies "Let me help you out," and walks away.

Ten minutes later, St. Peter calls to report that someone has set off a stink bomb and jammed the Pearly Gates so not a soul can escape the Hellish stench.

God commands, "Let Koutoukas in and give him whatever he wants."

So, to my atheist friends: possibly some quantum changes in store? After all, you can't spell "Him" without H. M.

Thank you, Harry, for the utter inability to be anyone other than your beautiful, flamboyant, caring, talented, hysterically funny self. I'll handle the sadness on my part.

Rest In Wit

I have to say it: Goodnight, sweet Diana Prince.

No Peers

insignificant droplets hardly qualify as tears
        yet wet
surely this life registers as one success after
        another
delirium replacing clear brilliance placeless
in a time of no cenacle no peers or academy
        to fight back

what can you do no one knows the difference
        Aristotle not the same
as if classical Greece was only an idea
        forgotten
standards hardly anyone appreciates thirty
        no forty years later

        Olympus
is a church worth worshipping
human values in a time of money first
        you write
and then you act it out
and then you go on being living
        how we all do go on

                      —Michael Smith

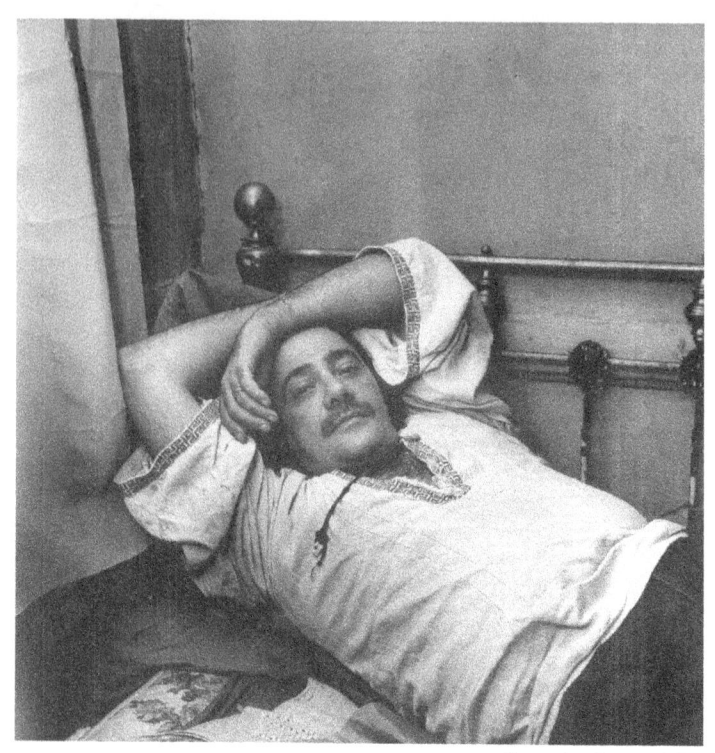

Photo by Peter Hujar

Documentation

The following is a first attempt to document the body of work by H. M. Koutoukas. The list is incomplete and dates may be disputable, but it begins to document Harry's creative genius. Sources include the Caffe Cino Collection in the Billy Rose Theatre Collection at the Lincoln Center Library for the Performing Arts; James D. Gossage archives; La Mama E.T.C. archives; Theater for the New City archives; Judson Poets' Theatre archives; Doollee Online Database; Lortel archives; Robert Patrick; and The New York Times. Very little information has so far been found for the years 1978-1988. —Magie Dominic

Known Plays by H. M. Koutoukas
(alphabetical list of titles)

1. *All Day for a Dollar, or Crumpled Christmas*

2. *Amphetamine Glamour*

3. *Atlantis and More*

4. *Awful People Are Coming Over So We Must Be Pretending to Be Hard at Work and Hope They Will Go Away*

5. *Black and Blue and Freezer Burned on Monday*

6. *The Book for Joel*

7. *Burglar on the Roof*

8. *Burglars and Bunglers*

9. *Butterfly Encounter*

10. *Cause Célèbre*

11. *The Children's Crusade*

12. *Christopher at Sheridan Squared*

13. *Cobra Invocations*

14. *Corn on the Cobb*

15. *Dead at Sea (a Collaboration)*
16. *Death by Desire*
17. *Enough Said the Custard Heart*
18. *Feathers Are for Ramming, or Tell Me Tender Tales*
19. *French Dressing (revue, written with others)*
20. *Grandmother Is in the Strawberry Patch*
21. *Hand Job for Apollo*
22. *Howard Kline Trilogy*
23. *Invocations of a Haunted Mind*
24. *Last Night I Dreamt I Was Julie Bravado*
25. *The Last Triangle (an Embroidered Camp)*
26. *A Letter from Colette, or Dreams Don't Send Valentines*
27. *The Machine That Couldn't*
28. *The Man Who Shot His Washing Machine*
29. *Medea, or Maybe the Stars May Understand (a Ritualistic Camp)*
30. *The Methedrine Madonna*
31. *Michael Touched Me*
32. *My Orpheus*
33. *Orny Queen of the Faeries (an Historic Camp)*
34. *One Man's Religion*
35. *Only a Countess May Dance When She's Crazy (an Historical Camp)*
36. *A Perfect Picture of Picture Perfect*
37. *The Pinotti Papers*
38. *Pomegranada*
39. *Pope Joan, or A Soul to Tweak (a Divine Camp)*
40. *Quicksilver*
41. *Ring of Death*

42. *Skin of the Night*
43. *Starflowers in an Ancient Land*
44. *Suicide Notations (a Play for Fire Escapes)*
45. *Theory for the Application of Rainbows*
46. *Tidy Passions, or Kill, Kaleidoscope, Kill (an Epic Camp)*
47. *Too Late for Yogurt*
48. *Turtles Don't Dream, or Happy Birthday, Jesus*
49. *The Ugliest Gargoyle*
50. *The View from Sorrento*
51. *When Clowns Play Hamlet*
52. *With Creatures Make My Way (a Bitter Camp)*

Production History

Only a Countess May Dance When She's Crazy (an Historical Camp

December 1964, January 5-24, 1965: Caffè Cino; directed by the author, assisted by Renée Maugin, with Carol Griffith as Countess Olie Samovitch, Renée Maugin as Screams; lighting by Dennis Parichy; hairstyles by Dina Harris; ribbons by Conrad Ward; gown by Betty Matta; special effects by Joe Davies. Revived in 1991; see *When Lightning Strikes Twice*.

The Last Triangle (an Embroidered Camp) and *Pope Joan, or A Soul to Tweak (a Divine Camp)*

March 15, 1965: Writer's Stage, as part of a benefit organized by Edward Albee (H. M. Koutoukas, Benefit Chair) for the Caffè Cino, which had been destroyed by a fire on March 3; directed by the author, with Nan Wilson as Pope Joan and Robert Schwartz as Jester; special effects by Joe Davies; Miss Wilson's gown by Abby Shahn; Miss Wilson's shoes by Robert Dahdah; benefit lighting by Dennis Parichy. *The Last Triangle* was revived November 2004: Know Theatre, Binghamton, New York.

With Creatures Make My Way (a Bitter Camp)
May 1965: Caffè Cino; directed by Roberta Sklar, with Warren Finnerty; lighting by John P. Dodd. Revived April 1967; directed by Michael Smith, with Charles Stanley.

Tidy Passions, or Kill, Kaleidoscope, Kill (an Epic Camp)
June 1965: La Mama; directed by the author, with Charles Stanley (as Jean Harlow), Linn Johnson, Tosh Carrillo, Mari-Claire Charba, Alice Turner, Andrew Sherwood, Jacque-Lynn Colton; music by Charles Stanley; technical coordinator: Ellen Levine. Published in *More Plays from Off-Off-Broadway*, edited by Michael Smith (Bobbs Merrill, 1972)

Omy Queen of the Faeries (an Historic Camp)
June 28-, 1965: La Mama; directed by the author, with Helen Hanft; music by Charles Stanley.

Feathers Are for Ramming, or Tell Me Tender Tales
September 23, 1965: Coda Galleries.

Medea, or Maybe the Stars May Understand, or Veiled Strangeness (a Ritualistic Camp)
October 13-17, 1965: La Mama; October 19-31, 1965: Caffè Cino; directed by the author, with Charles Stanley, Pat Holland, Daniel Davis; music by Robert Cosmos Savage; set by Kenneth Burgess. October 29-November 14: Theatre Genesis; directed by Warren Finnerty, with Linda Eskenas, Anthony Sciabona.

All Day for a Dollar, or Crumpled Christmas
December 1965: Caffè Cino; directed by the author, with Charles Stanley, Candace Scott, Robert Dahdah, and Ron Link; sets by Charles Stanley; lighting by John P. Dodd; movement by Deborah Lee; music by Robert Cosmos Savage. Revived in 1991; see *When Lightning Strikes Twice*.

Cause Célèbre
1966: Caffè Cino

A Letter from Colette, or Dreams Don't Send Valentines
February 15-26, 1966: Caffè Cino; directed by the author, with Mary Boylan and Edward Barton (Bhartonn); lighting by John P. Dodd. Revived December 1 and 10, 2006: Know Theatre, Binghamton, New York.

Pomegranada
March 1966: Judson Poets' Theatre; opera with music by Al Carmines; directed by Al Carmines, with Michael Elias, Julie Kurnitz, Burt Supree, David Vaughan, Margaret Wright, Walter Harris on drums, and Al Carmines at the piano. Also performed July 9, 1966, at the Sundance Festival, Upper Black Eddy, Pennsylvania.

Turtles Don't Dream, or Happy Birthday, Jesus, or Amphetamine Angel
February 4, 1966: Carnegie Recital Hall. Revived June 30-July 10, 1977: Theater for the New City; directed by the author, with Illa Howe, Gino de Fulgentiis, Mary Boylan, Joy Hattis; music by Robert Cosmos Savage and Tom O'Horgan; choreography by Gino de Fulgentiis; scenery by Mario Rivoli; lighting by Don McConnell.

The View from Sorrento
1967: Caffè Cino

When Clowns Play Hamlet
February 1967: La Mama; directed, designed, and choreographed by the author, with Jeff Weiss, Mary Boylan, Beverly Grant, and Tom O'Horgan; music by Robert Cosmos Savage; lighting by Dennis Parichy; elephant mural by Abby Shahn; technical coordinator Claris Nelson; costumes by Eugenia Louis.

Michael Touched Me
1967: Caffè Cino

The Book for Joel
April 10, 1967: Judson Memorial Church, as part of a Memorial Offering to Joe Cino.

The Machine That Couldn't
June 1967: 13th Street Theatre; directed by the author; choreography by Marjay, lighting by Charles Stanley, sets by Kenneth Burgess, music by Robert Cosmos Savage.

Two Camps by Koutoukas
March 18–April 2, 1968: Actors Playhouse; a double bill of *The Last Triangle (an Embroidered Camp)* and a revival of *Only a Countess May Dance When She's Crazy*; presented by Barbara Wise Productions, Inc.; directed by the author, with Gretel Cummings, Eddie McCarty, Aileen Passloff, Margaret Wright; musical director: Benji Heywood; incidental music by Robert Cosmos Savage; choreography by Aileen Passloff; costumes by Maria Irene Fornes; lighting by John P. Dodd.

Howard Kline Trilogy
1968: NYC.

Invocations of a Haunted Mind
October 31, 1969: Elgin Theatre; published in *The Off-Off-Broadway Book,* edited by Albert Poland and Bruce Mailman (Bobbs-Merrill, 1972).

Death by Desire and *Last Night I Dreamt I Was Julie Bravado*
November 1970: Elgin Theatre.

Christopher at Sheridan Squared
November 1971: Performing Garage; designed and directed by Donald L. Brooks, with Harvey Fierstein, Bryan Hayes; choreography by James Waring.

Suicide Notations (a Play for Fire Escapes)
October 22, 1972: fire escapes of Christopher Street; directed

by J. S. Hall, with Lisa Jane Persky, H. M. Koutoukas, Jackie Curtis, Taylor Mead, Ronald Tavel, James Hall, Ron Whyte, Jane Roberts; videotaped by Rudi Stern and the Global Village collective.

Grandmother Is in the Strawberry Patch
July 1973: La Mama; directed by the author, with Lisa Jane Persky, Benton Quin, Mary Boylan; music by Albert Fine. Also winter 2007: Know Theatre, Binghamton, New York.

French Dressing
1974: revue, written with others.
One Man's Religion and *The Pinotti Papers*
January 1975: La Mama; double bill.

Starflowers in an Ancient Land
December 25, 1975: La Mama; music by Tom O'Horgan and Gale Garnett.

Theory for the Application of Rainbows
September 1977: Circle Repertory Theatre; play for six characters written for memorial for Charles Stanley; cast included Magie Dominic.

Too Late for Yogurt
April 1978: Westbeth Theatre Center; directed by the author, with Mary Boylan, Ronnie Cooper, Bruce Eyster, Peter Hulit, Russell Krum, Viva Welles; scenery by Peter Hulit; lighting by Carol Grubner.

The Butterfly Encounter
1978: Theater for the New City; music by David Forman.

The Ugliest Gargoyle
January 16, 1987: Astor Place Playhouse; directed by the author, with Russell Krum.

Hand Job for Apollo
1988: NYC

When Lightning Strikes Twice
January 1991: Charles Ludlam Theatre; double bill of *Awful People Are Coming Over So We Must Pretend to Be Hard at Work and Hope They Will Go Away* and a revival of *Only a Countess May Dance When She's Crazy*; presented by the Ridiculous Theatrical Company; directed by Eureka, with Everett Quinton; set by Tom Moore; costumes by Daniel Boike; lighting by Richard Currie; props by Vicky Raab; jewelry by Wendy Gell; production stage manager: James Eckerle; music and sound by Mark Bennett. Published by Samuel French. *Awful People...* was also presented in 2003 by Know Theatre, Binghamton, New York.

Skin of the Night
October 8-, 1992: La Mama; directed by the author, with Deborah Braun, Giselle Liberatore, Stewart A. Gardner, Maggie Low, Ann Harris, Robert Lanier, Jean-Claude Vasseux, and John Edward Heys.

Enough Said the Custard Heart
December 1993: Theater for the New City; directed by the author; scenery by Richard Kordtz and Richard Currie; costumes by Carol Tauser.

Dead at Sea
April 27, 1999: Dixon Place; a performance in collaboration with Thom Fogarty based on H. M. Koutoukas's journals.

The Man Who Shot His Washing Machine
January 25-February 18, 2001: Theater for the New City.

Corn on the Cobb
April 2001: Theater for the New City.

A Perfect Picture of Picture Perfect
February 20-March 9, 2003: Theater for the New City.

Ring of Death
June 10-27, 2004: Theater for the New City; directed by Maggie Low, with Florence Young; costumes by Carol Tauser.

Quicksilver
November-December 2005: Know Theatre, Binghamton, New York.

Published Plays

Invocations of a Haunted Mind
in *The Off-Off-Broadway Book: The Plays, People, Theatre*, by Albert Poland and Bruce Mailman; Bobbs-Merrill, 1972.

Tidy Passions, or Kill, Kaleidoscope, Kill
in *More Plays from Off-Off-Broadway*, edited by Michael Smith; Bobbs-Merrill, 1972.

Awful People Are Coming Over So We Must Be Pretending to Be Hard at Work and Hope They Will Go Away and *Only a Countess May Dance When She's Crazy*
in *When Lightning Strikes Twice*; Samuel French, 1991.

Medea of the Laundromat, or The Stars May Understand
in *Return to the Caffè Cino,* edited by Steve Susoyev and George Birimisa; Moving Finger Press, 2007.

Awards

National Arts Club Award for Experimental Playwriting, for *The Last Triangle*, 1965.

Obie Award from *The Village Voice*; Special Citation "for the style and energy of his assaults on the theatre in both playwriting and production," 1966.

Chesley Playwriting Award from The Publishing Triangle, New York, 2003.

Relevant Books
referencing H. M. Koutoukas, Caffè Cino, and Off-Off-Broadway

Theatre Journal, Winter 1967, by Michael Smith; University of Missouri Press, 1967

Joseph Cino and the First Off-Off-Broadway Theater, article by Douglas W. Gordy in *Passing Performances: Queer Readings of Leading Players in American Theatre History*, edited by Robert A. Schanke and Kimberley Bell Marra; University of Michigan Press, 1998.

Greenwich Village 1963: Avant-Garde Performance and the Effervescent Body, by Sally Banes; Duke University Press, 1999.

The Queen of Peace Room, by Magie Dominic; Wilfrid Laurier University Press, 2002.

Off-Off-Broadway Explosion: How Provocative Playwrights of the 1960s Ignited a New American Theater, by David A. Crespy, with a Foreword by Edward Albee; Back Stage Books, 2003.

Playing Underground: A Critical History of the 1960s Off-Off-Broadway Movement, by Stephen J. Bottoms; University of Michigan Press, 2004.

The Oxford Companion to American Theatre; article on Caffè Cino by G. Bordman and T. S. Hischak; Oxford University Press, 2004.

Caffè Cino: The Birthplace of Off-Off-Broadway, by Wendell C. Stone; Southern Illinois University Press, 2005.

Return to the Caffè Cino, edited by Steve Susoyev and George Birimisa; Moving Finger Press, 2007.

The Gay and Lesbian Theatrical Legacy: A Biographical Dictionary of Major Figures in American Stage History in the Pre-Stonewall Era, edited by Billy J. Harbin, Kimberley Bell Marra, and Robert A. Schanke; University of Michigan Press, 2005.

Libraries & Archives

Billy Rose Theatre Collection, Lincoln Center Library for the Performing Arts: James D. Gossage Photo Collection; Caffè Cino Collection.

Rutgers University Archives: Special Collections.

New York University, Elmer Holmes Bobst Library: Fales Library and Special Collections; 3 ID: 232.0013, Harry Koutoukas Oral History; interviewed by Kait Medley, November 11, 2008. Richard Hell Papers Collection: three collaborative poems by Cookie Mueller and H. M. Koutoukas: *At the Hour Before Dawn, Keep a Few Things in Mind*, and *Those Days*, 1981.

www.ingramcontent.com/pod-product-compliance
Lightning Source LLC
Chambersburg PA
CBHW032133090426
42743CB00007B/581